'What better recommendation is there than to say that a number of MD2MD members have adopted Pete's simple but effective toolkit to focus their own team's actions'
Bob Bradley, Chairman, MD2MD

'Pete's *Unstoppable* system has been invaluable in helping me establish very clear personal and business goals, keeping me highly focused on the actions necessary to achieve success'
Lee Quarzi, Finance Director, Harlands Accountants

'Without the *Unstoppable* process we could still be trying to do everything at once. The process has brought The MPA Group company-wide clarity on where we need to prioritise our efforts to achieve our business vision'
Dave Pepper, Director, The MPA Group

'Without a doubt I would recommend Pete Wilkinson to anyone who is serious about improving their business and life, take action and contact Pete it's the best thing I have ever done'
David Wilkinson, DH Fitness www.dhfitness.com

'Probably my most worthwhile 4hrs of the year! Great adrenalin rush of self-positivity. Immediate reaction, great feeling'
Keith Robson, IDT Ltd, www.usedcomputerstore.co.uk

'Positive Pete Wilkinson is undoubtedly the most motivated person I have ever worked with, his enthusiasm and charisma is such a joy to work to with. Pete has had a huge positive effect on me, my working attitude and my business'
Helenlee Whalley, Creator of The Instant FitPro Product

'If you are looking to improve yourself as well as your business, then you should certainly attend one of Pete's seminars'
Neil Todd, Owner, T.H. Todd & Associates

'If you need inspiration to do things better, then this is it. Arrive with an empty notebook but leave with one bursting with ideas. Highly recommend'
Ron Clarke, Media and PR Consultant, Northfield Communications

'Pete is a business Mr Motivator, mixed with your old Headmaster – so watch out if you don't do your homework! I thought I was pretty motivated already, but this was like being propelled up a steep mountain with a sharp stick'
Kate Slater, Kate Slater PR and Marketing www.kspr.co.uk

'I can't recommend Pete highly enough, he is superb at motivating and helping you achieve your goals. Do yourself a favour, book him immediately! You won't regret it if you're serious about increasing your business'
Ken Robson, Owner, Ace Mortgage Consultants

'I have seen Pete deliver his keynote presentation on many occasions. His unbridled energy, focus and drive combined with Pete's own 1-3-5 structure provide a powerful cocktail that is guaranteed to capture the attention of any audience'
Dan Bond, Presentation & Business Development Specialist

UNSTOPPABLE

Using the power of focus to take action and achieve your goals

Pete Wilkinson

CAPSTONE
A Wiley Brand

This edition first published 2015
© 2015 Pete Wilkinson

Registered office

John Wiley and Sons Ltd, The Atrium, Southern Gate, Chichester, West Sussex, PO19 8SQ,
United Kingdom

For details of our global editorial offices, for customer services and for information about
how to apply for permission to reuse the copyright material in this book please see our
website at www.wiley.com.

Wiley publishes in a variety of print and electronic formats and by print-on-demand.
Some material included with standard print versions of this book may not be included in
e-books or in print-on-demand. If this book refers to media such as a CD or DVD
that is not included in the version you purchased, you may download this material at
http://booksupport.wiley.com. For more information about Wiley products, visit
www.wiley.com.

Designations used by companies to distinguish their products are often claimed as
trademarks. All brand names and product names used in this book and on its cover are
trade names, service marks, trademark or registered trademarks of their respective
owners. The publisher and the book are not associated with any product or vendor
mentioned in this book. None of the companies referenced within the book have
endorsed the book.

Library of Congress Cataloging-in-Publication Data
Wilkinson, Pete
Unstoppable : using the power of focus to take action and achieve your goals / Pete
Wilkinson.
    pages cm
  ISBN 978-0-857-08582-5 (pbk.)
1. Success in business. 2. Success. 3. Motivation (Psychology) 4. Goal (Psychology) I. Title.
  HF5386.W4975 2015
  650.1—dc23   2014030760

A catalogue record for this book is available from the British Library.

ISBN 978-0-857-08582-5 (paperback)   ISBN 978-0-857-08584-9 (ebk)
ISBN 978-0-857-08583-2 (ebk)

Cover design: Wiley
Cover image: © Shutterstock.com/Eky Studio

Set in 11/14pt MyriadPro-Regular by Laserwords Private Limited, Chennai, India
Printed in Great Britain by TJ International Ltd, Padstow, Cornwall, UK

To my gorgeous wife Sharon and my three beautiful daughters Megan, Molly and Maya. This book has been a huge challenge for me and without their support I could not have completed it.

Contents

Preface

The castle looked beautiful in the morning sunshine standing high and proud on the hill. The lake was calm with tiny ripples tickling the shoreline. We all stood ready to enter, nervously wondering what was going to happen next.

I'd been up since 3.30am; I'd had a massive breakfast because I knew it was going to be a long day.

At 5.50am I stepped into the lake and, even though it was August, as the cold water filled my wetsuit it took my breath away and I clumsily swam to get fully submerged.

After sharing a few words with the people next to me it all suddenly changed. At 6am the klaxon sounded and within minutes the calm start was a distant memory. I was literally getting kicked and punched by the other competitors – it was sheer pandemonium. My first goal was to just reach the first buoy without panicking and sinking to the bottom.

I managed to get out of the water 2 minutes ahead of my target time, driving myself on to start the 112-mile bike leg.

After about 7 hours taking in each long mile, I was back in transition and changed into my running gear getting ready for a full 26.2-mile marathon (just what you want the most, having already been racing for about 8 hours).

I'd done the training and paid the entrance fee and was determined to finish the race. I was discovering new levels of fatigue but as I finally crossed the finishing line, I realized that it's at moments like this that you discover the person you really are.

Discovering who you really are is one of the main reasons I love to compete in long-distance triathlons and cycle events. We are goal-seeking mechanisms. I think the reason why so many people don't make the most of themselves is because they don't habitually set goals. When you set yourself a goal, a real challenge that requires you to commit to in order to be successful, you connect with the person you really are. You tap into areas of your personality that you forgot about. You demonstrate resolve and tenacity, skills that are there but often dormant. In short, when you start to perform at your best in order to complete a goal, you become alive.

The only reason I was able to complete this huge challenge was because I became Unstoppable. Just imagine what you will achieve when you perform at your best, make the most of yourself and you become Unstoppable?

Part One

The Beginning

1

Why Develop an Unstoppable Attitude?

When you compete in a challenge like an Ultra Endurance Triathlon you have to be quite fit. But you don't even stand a chance of reaching the finish line inside the 17-hour cut-off without realizing that your mindset can dramatically affect your attitude.

I've read a lot of quotes about mindset and attitude. One of my favourite ones is:

Attitude is the little thing that makes the big difference.

While being a company sales manager and to a lesser extent when I had my own retail business, I had to conduct lots of interviews. One of the key areas I used to focus on was to appoint for attitude and train for skill. So, if a candidate had the right attitude but didn't have all the necessary skills, they would still be ahead of the candidate from a competitor company that displayed the wrong attitude.

I'm sure you have been into a store, bank or medical surgery and a member of staff displayed the wrong type of attitude. From my experience, I've felt like I was interrupting that person. You can then turn the corner and visit another business and have a completely different experience. I've even walked into a train station and met two people from the same business that gave me a completely different experience of the business. It's amazing to consider that some businesses don't address these traits. Attitude really is the little thing that makes the big difference.

Going back to the Ultra Endurance Triathlon as an example, you develop your mindset over the months of training you do. You also develop your mindset by training in bad weather in the depths of winter. You have to work on your mental strength because completing a 140-mile race tests your mental strength as much as your physical strength. So, during your 20-week training programme you have to build the mindset that will develop the attitude that you can complete the event comfortably. OK, you may be a little uncomfortable towards the end, but you get the picture.

There are lots of components that come into play when you are developing your attitude for endurance racing. You have to consider your nutrition, your physical training, your mental strength training in winter and dealing with setbacks such as mechanical failure with your bike. There is also dealing with missed training sessions because of work commitments or family. All of these go into the pot of building the attitude that you will be successful on the day of the race and reach the finishing line in one piece.

The same approach applies when developing your attitude for your business and life. I believe that where you are now is a result of all the thoughts that occupied your mind and the actions that you took up to this point.

I believe that where you are now is not where you **Where you are now is not** have to stay. I know that change is inevitable but **where you have to stay.** growth is optional. You are the one person who can decide how you respond to that change. If you look around I'm sure you can find people and companies that failed to respond effectively to that change: you can be different.

The fact that you are reading this shows me that you are prepared to try something different. I'm going to share with you the seven components that make up the full Unstoppable system. You will build your mindset, become more confident and approach your business and life challenges with certainty. Because of these changes you will set bigger and bigger goals and live a bigger life.

One of the greatest characteristics of winners is that they develop the expectation of success way before there is any evidence to support that success is certain. They simply believe that they will be successful. I received a reply recently from Tom Peters (business speaker and author of *In Search of Excellence*, www.tompeters.com) on Twitter (I have to say I was humbled and thrilled, I studied Tom loads during business school). He said that belief is pointless without the right toolkit. Well, part of the benefit of an Unstoppable system is that you are going to build the right toolkit in Part 3 where we develop the key skills. You'll then learn how to put the skills together and develop a 1-3-5 Action Plan, which will massively improve your results.

Right now at the beginning you may not have a certain positive mindset that you can achieve the level of success you want. When you start out you say to yourself 'right, this is going to be tough, can I do it?' Then with time as you train and practice consistently your belief and confidence grow. As your belief and confidence grows your toolkit grows. It is OK to be unsure at first, developing your Unstoppable system is an exciting journey; admittedly very challenging at times but still exciting. I'm not going to say that you can develop your Unstoppable system overnight – you can't – it will take a little time. But I am going to show you how by developing your mindset you can dramatically affect your attitude.

1. You are going to develop 1 Crystal Clear Vision of what a successful life and business looks like and sounds like to you. This Vision will clearly and succinctly describe where you want to be and give you an overall focus.

2. You will develop 3 Core Objectives that will chunk down your Vision so that you keep on track and stop doing what many business owners and professionals do, which is chase bright blue butterflies.

3. You will establish 5 action orientated Goals for each core objective so that you have a daily focus. I will show you how to identify the tasks that are needed to complete your 5 Goals. By focusing on your 5 Goals you will achieve your Core Objectives. Then by achieving your 3 Core Objectives you will achieve your Vision.

4. You will develop your Leadership Skills so that you become a far more effective leader, even if the only person you lead is yourself!

5. You will develop your Personal Organization so that you make the very best of your 86,400 seconds every day.

6. You will develop your Relationship Skills focusing on the relationship and not just the transaction.

7. You will develop your Key Strengths and learn to manage and delegate your weaknesses so that you dramatically increase your effectiveness within your business.

When you have developed your foundation 1-3-5 Action Plan (1 Vision, 3 Core Objectives and 5 Goals for each Core Objective) and then developed the key skills to maximize the application **By developing your mindset you can dramatically affect your attitude.** of your 1-3-5, you will be far more confident, your belief will increase and you will have developed your Unstoppable system.

I remember how I felt when I entered the biggest physical challenge of my life, my first Ultra Endurance Triathlon. I was absolutely terrified. I had never undertaken anything like it before and that scared me. There were times in preparing for this challenge that I doubted I could achieve it. I knew I would only finish it if I was focused and consistent in my preparation.

Just as I faced my Ultra Endurance challenge, I bet you have some challenges you are facing right now. I'm sure that in your life, your work or your business you've thought about those challenges but for some reason you haven't followed through yet. **Your attitude can dramatically effect the thoughts you have, the feelings you experience and the actions you take.**

I imagine something has prevented you from progressing; maybe you didn't know where to start. I know what that feels like, and I know what it feels like to achieve that challenge. It is certainly worth the effort.

Your attitude can dramatically effect the thoughts you have, the feelings you experience and the actions you take.

The way to achieve whatever challenge you are facing is to develop an Unstoppable attitude and implement your Unstoppable system.

How it all works

This book is split into four main parts. Part One is The Beginning and where you are right now. Its purpose is to set the scene and share with you what is possible when you become Unstoppable.

Part Two is The Foundation and focuses on the 1-3-5 Action Plan and how to create your own so you have a framework to become Unstoppable.

Part Three is all about The Execution Skills. As I've said, having your 1-3-5 Action Plan is not enough; the magic happens when you begin to use it.

Part Four is sharing with you how to have a fantastic next 12 months using your plan and also reviewing the main areas of your life and business.

Throughout the book I will share anecdotal stories about what others, including myself, have done to meet our challenges and how these relate to you. Also, I want to share what you can achieve when you answer the number one important question: 'If I was the very best version of myself, what could I achieve?'

I have also highlighted some other 'Key Questions' for you to answer and to get you thinking. In addition to this I will give you 'Key Development Points' for you to note, which will be your 'takeaways'.

I am very passionate about you developing your Unstoppable system. I have seen first hand, many times, the difference it makes to people's lives, business and careers. It is very important that you stick with me until we reach the end of the book. It's a bit like a jigsaw that fits together and then you'll see the whole picture.

The Birth of the 1-3-5 Action Plan

I've spent years studying strategy stuff. When I was completing my MBA at business school we seemed to explore every conceivable strategy. Now, at the risk of sounding a little controversial and even possibly upsetting some of my clients (I work with a great deal of accountants), in my opinion business plans are not written as ongoing working documents. Most seem to be written with a single purpose in mind at the start but are not referred to during the everyday work on the front line.

What you need then is a simple plan that's easy to follow and easy to stick with. It must be clear about where you are going, what you're going to focus on to get there and what the goals are that can chart your progress and track your actions.

Enter my (and very soon to be your own) 1-3-5 Action Plan. Your 1-3-5 will motivate you to take daily action on the most rewarding and profitable things that will absolutely accelerate your progress. When you create and then 'live' your 1-3-5 you'll start to achieve more in a week than most drifting (possibly you before) business owners do in a month.

Your 1-3-5 will enable you to achieve better results. I'm not saying it's easy but it's worth it.

Alan Wigham, Director from Safeguard Commercial Finance, completed his Unstoppable system and said:

> *Pete's programme has made me realize that my Core Objectives and Goals are fundamental in the business and they must be revisited regularly if I am to achieve my Vision, they cannot stay still, as in the current age; to stay still is to go backwards! To summarize, interesting yes, a little uncomfortable yes, challenging yes, but worth it? YES.*

So in answer to my opening question and the title of this chapter 'Why Develop an Unstoppable Attitude?', I think it's very clear. You have challenges in your life, business and career that you are facing right now and by becoming Unstoppable you'll meet these challenges and achieve your full potential. Ultimately you'll live the life you deserve!

I bet you are motivated now!

Part Two

The Foundation

2

Becoming Effective is All About Your Habits!

Having a solid foundation is critical to the success of your life and business. When I made the decision to complete an Ultra Endurance Triathlon I realized from my experience in business and from business school that I needed a plan. I also realized that I needed a simple plan, one that I could follow. I wanted to set myself up to succeed. Many people start a business without giving enough attention to the foundation upon which it is built. I'm sure you've heard of the phrase 'built on shifting sand'. Come on, be honest, there's just you and me; how much time have you given to your business foundation?

The Eiffel Tower in Paris is a beautiful site. Standing at the bottom and looking up at its 1063-foot structure is awe inspiring. If you haven't had a meal in its high level restaurant, I would certainly recommend it.

The tower was built by the engineer Gustave Eiffel, and one French mathematics professor thought it would collapse at a height of 748 feet. It was thought also that it would only last 20 years; it's still standing strong over 100 years later.

One of the main reasons the tower is still a beacon of French pride is because of how Eiffel designed its foundation. Gustave intricately designed the tower's foundation, which is composed of cement and stone placed at an exact angle so that each of the four curved piers of the tower with an inward tilt of 54 degrees would maximize wind resistance and exert a perpendicular thrust to its foundation. In addition, the legs of the tower rested on sand boxes and hydraulic jacks during construction so that the metal beams at the tower's first platform could be levelled within one millimetre of the horizontal plane. (*Yale Scientific*, 12 May 2011, www.yalescientific.org)

So, it is fair to say that the level of focus and detail that Gustave Eiffel displayed in designing the tower is the key reason why it is still standing today. What can we learn from this?

What I am suggesting is that you look at your business and your life and build a similar style solid foundation. If you have a large business that has departments, what are the foundations like within those departments? The physical training you do when preparing for an Endurance Triathlon is all part of building a foundation so that you are able to move at pace consistently for up to 17 hours. I know for certain that when you do build that solid foundation your business will be more stable, more profitable and far more successful.

But most people don't do that. Most people have a notion of what they want to achieve, a vague idea of what success looks like and just start the process of delivering. I'm not saying taking action isn't vital; it is and I always look to execute my ideas – plus I'm constantly working on getting better at this. What I am saying is that most business owners come in on a Monday morning and just start doing what they have always done largely in the same way and expect a different result. That is not going to happen. This way of approaching your business is opportunistic. If you want to be successful in your business or even in general life, you need to get strategic! If you want a nice weekend away, you have to plan it. If you want your child to have a lovely birthday party, you have to plan it. If you want to achieve double-digit growth this year in your business, you have to plan it. It's a fact that most people spend more time planning their annual 2-week family holiday than their business or role within a business.

If you want to be successful in your business or even in general life, you need to get strategic!

Key Question

What is the number one goal you are currently working towards?

Completing an Ultra Endurance Triathlon was a really big achievement for me. It was the hardest physical thing I've ever undertaken, and the training is also very hard. In fact, getting to the start line in one piece is a challenge in itself. During my training plan I had to remain focused, and with Ultra Endurance training you have to be consistent.

During the first week I did 8 hours of training, which is quite substantial but it was only the start. By the time I reached the peak week, which was 5 weeks before the race, I would be training 18 hours a week! On my peak week I swam 4000 metres on Monday, rode 6 hours and 100 miles on Wednesday and then ran for 3 hours covering 18 miles on Friday! This was in addition to another five tough sessions.

Yes, other people have completed them more often and do them in a faster time. The point I want to make is that doing an Ultra Endurance

Triathlon was me pushing myself and testing my limits. For you it may be a 10k run, a double Triathlon or learning a challenging new skill or language. The key is that you push yourself to shift out of your comfort zone. That's where the development comes. All too often we get comfortable in our lives and our businesses. When we get comfortable we can start to coast. That's the absolute worst thing that can happen to a high performance person like you and me. We need to be pushed and we need to be challenged. Have a look around you now and see if you are comfortable. If you are, set a challenge, sign up for an event, a course or commit to a new level of performance.

Key Development Point

The last thing you want to do is flick your cruise control switch.

Stretch goals are a great way to make sure you don't flick your cruise control switch. What stretch goal could you set right now that you will complete in the next 90 days? A stretch goal is something that when you achieve it, it will deliver a quantum shift in performance for you or your business. It might be launching a new product, writing a book, learning an instrument or acquiring a new strategically significant client (someone who is ideal and really gets what you do and will pay you the correct fee). Email your stretch goal to pete@petewilkinson.com with the subject title 'My 90-day stretch' and let me know what you're going to achieve. When you set a 90-day stretch goal that engages you and means you really have to commit, you'll feel alive. That is what we need to continually push ourselves and raise our limits.

❗ Key Development Point

Begin the habit of setting 90-day stretch goals. You'll love the progress you'll make. We're often overambitious about what we can achieve in a day or a week and underambitious about what we can achieve in 3 months or a year.

There were times during the run in my Triathlon that I asked myself 'why am I doing this?' and the answer was always the same 'because you can, because you need to'. Towards the end of the race I had a beautiful, clear vision of me reaching the finish line by 7.30pm, once again being back in the grounds of Sherborne Castle. The same castle that stood high on the hill at 6am in the morning when the race started and everything became a frantic rush of activity. I'd see my wife when I reached the finish chute and that euphoric feeling would make all the training and all the effort seem worthwhile. I'd cross the finishing line and hear 'Pete Wilkinson, you are an Ultra Endurance Triathlete.' I'd then have the medal placed around my neck. Then the pain would stop and I could eat some proper food! That is why my focus wasn't on the pain I was experiencing during the race; it was on the way I would feel at the end.

All too often when we're doing something difficult or when we consider doing something difficult, we often focus on the feeling while immersed in the task instead of the great feeling we'll experience when we've completed the task.

If instead you aim to build the habit of connecting to the outcome rather than to the task, you will take more action on what you need to take action on and achieve more. You have to develop the strength to control what thoughts occupy your mind if you want to be successful. Sometimes you have to take emotion out of the equation.

When running a business there are things that are going to be fun. Setting up a new office, business premises or launching a new product can be fun. Building a fantastic team and seeing it gel and grow can be fun; I've recently experienced this myself. Smashing your year one sales target can be fun. But there are things that absolutely have to be done that aren't fun. Sometimes you just have to write that report, sometimes you just have to follow up with those notes after the meeting and sometimes you have to get to the office sharp and get stuck in to that difficult task!

When you get control of the thoughts that occupy your mind and keep focused on the positive ones, you'll get momentum on your side and make far more effective progress. There have been three races where I wanted to stop. There have been times in my business when challenge after challenge made me want to stop. The thoughts that occupied my mind at the time were 'you can't go on, you're too tired' and 'why are there more and more challenges?' But you can go on, you can get control of your thoughts, you can switch them to be positive (focusing on your Vision really helps) and you can get through it.

Aren't there times in business when you're facing a tough challenge? Aren't there times in business when you're getting kicked and punched by your fellow competitors? Aren't there times in business and life where you shouldn't focus on what you are doing that is making you uncomfortable but focus on what your outcome is going to be? Learn to control the thoughts that occupy your mind; be focused and consistent and you'll be Unstoppable.

Triathlon links perfectly with everyday life in business. We all need to be multi-skilled, but being good at what you do is not enough, it's how you do it. If you are like most of the businesses that I work with there are many people in the same sector targeting the same sort of customers.

Your competitors are probably very good at what they do, just like you. But how you do what you do can make the difference between success and mediocrity.

How you do what you do can make the difference between success and mediocrity.

I have developed and distilled this Unstoppable system so that it can produce success in everyday life. I'm going to share everything with you here in this book so that you can develop your own Unstoppable system and then share it with your team, your support network and even your customers.

One of the key reasons why you will be having super busy days but not super effective days is because your plan is not sound. You may be like the many individuals I've already talked to and not actually have a plan. At a basic level you need to start with an idea of what success looks like, the outcome that you would like to achieve. When you form the habit of doing this on a daily basis and make sure every day counts in some way, then you'll be making more progress than you thought was possible.

Dr Tom Barratt (president of Business Life/Management, www.daretodream .net) says that we should not confuse busyness with business. I think this one simple statement sums up a great deal. You'll have seen people attend networking events, working on their social media or making some phone calls. They are confusing busyness with business. In business I believe we need to focus on producing a result. The clearer the result we want, the more likely we are to achieve that result. It's the same with your life in general; most people don't have the life they want because they are not clear what sort of life they want!

Key Development Point

Vague focus produces vague results.

So if your business or job is going to provide you with all the wonderful things you want in your life, don't they deserve you spending some time and designing a solid foundation so that they will deliver sustainable results for you for many years?

As I mentioned earlier, the first three key components here form your foundation and your massively powerful 1-3-5 Action Plan. These are the areas that we're going to work on first. We'll build a solid foundation and your 1-3-5 (1 Vision, 3 Core Objectives, 5 Goals for each Core Objective) will shape how you spend your time, ensure you make the most of your skills and direct your everyday focus so you always, absolutely always, make progress!

When I was training up to 18 hours a week for my Ultra Endurance Triathlon I set up and then followed a 1-3-5 Action Plan. It might not have been perfect then but I had a clear Vision of what I wanted to achieve. I also had 3 Core Objectives, one for each stage of the race, and 5 Goals that fed into my 3 Core Objectives.

Take a look at my 1-3-5 Action Plan overleaf.

This 1-3-5 is not as clear as my business one now, but I wanted to have some way of keeping focused and consistently training to achieve my Vision of standing on the finishing line by 7.30pm. You'll find that in the early stages as you build your 1-3-5 you'll make slight changes to it – that's fine. It may not be right for you straight away, but you'll get there.

First things first

Before we can get started with building your 1-3-5 Action Plan, we first need to look at how you are operating currently. If 47% of what we do is habitual, it's important that we assess our habits and rituals and check

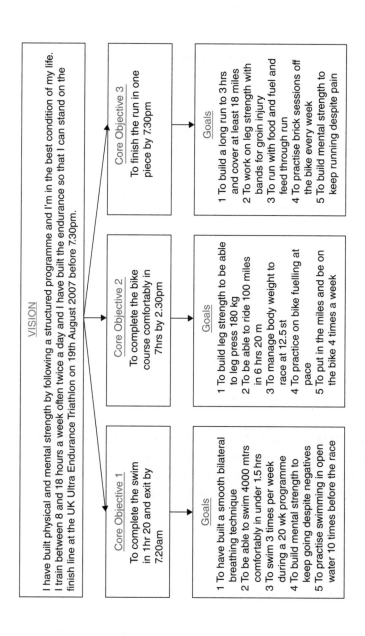

VISION

I have built physical and mental strength by following a structured programme and I'm in the best condition of my life. I train between 8 and 18 hours a week often twice a day and I have built the endurance so that I can stand on the finish line at the UK Ultra Endurance Triathlon on 19th August 2007 before 7.30pm.

Core Objective 1
To complete the swim in 1hr 20 and exit by 7.20am

Goals
1 To have built a smooth bilateral breathing technique
2 To be able to swim 4000 mtrs comfortably in under 1.5 hrs
3 To swim 3 times per week during a 20 wk programme
4 To build mental strength to keep going despite negatives
5 To practise swimming in open water 10 times before the race

Core Objective 2
To complete the bike course comfortably in 7hrs by 2.30pm

Goals
1 To build leg strength to be able to leg press 180 kg
2 To be able to ride 100 miles in 6 hrs 20 m
3 To manage body weight to race at 12.5st
4 To practice on bike fuelling at pace
5 To put in the miles and be on the bike 4 times a week

Core Objective 3
To finish the run in one piece by 7.30pm

Goals
1 To build a long run to 3 hrs and cover at least 18 miles
2 To work on leg strength with bands for groin injury
3 To run with food and fuel and feed through run
4 To practise brick sessions off the bike every week
5 To build mental strength to keep running despite pain

if they're serving or strangling us, because being effective is all about your habits.

A habit is something that we do on a regular basis until it becomes so easy that we can do it without thinking. It's behaviour (good or bad) that we do repeatedly until it becomes automatic. What about your habits?

Some of your habits will be good and some will be not so good. We need to get a clear starting point, so in the following space write the five good habits you have that are serving you. These could be things like being on time, finishing projects, communicating to your team or recording your business progress.

1 _____

2 _____

3 _____

4 _____

5 _____

Next, I'd like you to write a benefit for each of the good habits. What is the result or outcome that you experience because of this good habit? If a good habit was communicating to your team, then a benefit of this would be that your team is engaged and brings you ideas to improve the overall business.

1 _____

2 _____

3 _____

4 _____

5 _____

Now the uncomfortable bit, write the five bad habits you have that you know are not serving you. These may be obvious like smoking or drinking too much, or they may be not so obvious like always saying yes and taking on too much (one of my old ones). The reason we're doing this is because your bad habits will be influencing your performance and by identifying them means we can do something about them.

1 _____

2 _____

3 _____

4 _____

5 _____

Like before, list the five ways in which these are affecting you. I did this exercise recently with a client and one of their bad habits meant that they had to work late every night because they procrastinated in the morning. We came up with a solution to prevent the morning procrastination and they finished consistently at 5.30pm. Sometimes subtle changes result in great results.

1 _____

2 _____

3 _____

4 _____

5 _____

It takes about 21 days to form a new habit. I'd like you to look through your good habits and make sure that you have your life and business set up to keep practising your good habits. So, if you shave on a night before a very early breakfast meeting to save valuable minutes in the morning, what can you do to ensure you have the time to shave on a night? We'll start with the little stuff first (again one of my new successful habits).

Over now to the bad habits. It's possible before you did this little exercise that you weren't aware of what your bad habits were. Hopefully, now that they're out in the open, you want to do something about them.

If one of your bad habits is that you never finish anything or that you have the habit of seeing why something won't work instead of seeing how it could work, you need to be aware of it. If you kept repeating that habit and sorting for bad (sorting for bad is where a person sometimes without realizing only sees why something won't work. They are focusing only on the bad things that could happen or are happening not on what the possibilities could be), always finding ways why things won't work rather than being solution focused, you could be wasting your time reading this book. If you are not going to follow through and make it part of 'what you habitually do', building your 1-3-5 Action Plan foundation and then your full Unstoppable system will also be wasted effort.

If you kept repeating the bad habit of not finishing things, you may not finish this book and complete your 1-3-5 Action Plan. If you kept the bad habit of seeing why something won't work you may not even give your 1-3-5 Action Plan the chance to work!

Address these bad habits or others that you have and you'll open up a whole new range of possibilities for you to use your strengths.

You need to form the habit of finishing things and looking for the positive in whatever you do.

It's worth remembering that successful people have successful habits. A simple thing that I started a few years back is ensuring that every business quarter I focus on developing a new successful habit. I sit and think for a while about who I respect in business and life. I think about what they do (their habits and rituals) that enables them to be successful. I then build a picture of me (a simple Vision) having and displaying that habit. I really get emotionally connected to the benefits I'll experience by having that habit. I then set up my life, often by making simple subtle changes so that I can develop that habit. I pick a new habit to focus on every business quarter. Each year I develop at least four new habits.

Successful people have successful habits.

Now I want you to sit for a short while and think about someone who you respect and who is successful in an area you admire. Think about their habits and rituals that enable them to be successful. Then picture yourself having developed one of these habits as part of what you do. I want you to really get emotionally connected to the benefit you will experience in your life by developing this new successful habit. Once you have that connection, think about what simple changes you can make to develop that habit. Just imagine what you will achieve when you do this exercise every quarter and develop four new successful habits every single year!

In a business career of 30–40 years that's a lot of successful habit forming.

I want to stress here that some, even most, of these habits are not massive life-changing rituals on their own. Often it's what Darren Hardy (best-selling author and publisher of *Success* magazine, www.darrenhardy. com) refers to as 'The Compound Effect'. In his excellent programme, Darren talks about his success formula: Small smart choices + time + consistency = radical improvement. Each of my successful habits builds on the previous and in a very short time I'm performing better. Some of the successful habits I've developed recently include:

- Always calling people back within a certain time.

- Planning my time better by estimating how long tasks will take.

- Not relying on 'no traffic' and perfect green lights to get to meetings on time.

- Studying rather than just reading books. I record a brief summary in my journal.

- Only listening to personal development CDs in my car between 8am Monday and 6pm Friday.

- Giving genuine compliments to people I meet at networking events as well as colleagues and friends.

- Recording daily what I'm grateful for (an attitude of gratitude).

- Measuring my net worth on a monthly basis to ensure that it's increasing.

- Implementing a social media strategy with help from an expert rather than doing it blind (that's what I used to do).

- Continuously practising 'outcome thinking' so I always know what outcome I'd like from every action and interaction.

- Getting to meetings and networking events early to meet and chat with the other attendees.

I think you get the picture!

In the excellent book *The Power of Focus* by Jack Canfield, Mark Victor Hansen and Les Hewitt, the authors share what they call 'The Successful Habits Formula'. Briefly the formula is:

A: Identify the habit that is holding you back and the consequence of this habit.

B: Write what the successful new habit would be to replace the bad habit and a clear benefit of this habit.

C: Then identify three easy steps to jump-start the new habit.

The example they use is as follows:

A: Taking too much work home at weekends. Makes you feel guilty and restricts family time, damages relationships.

B: Completely free up weekends from work. Be more relaxed and feel rejuvenated, reduce stress and have new family experiences.

C: (1) Design your work better by not overcommitting. (2) Delegate secondary tasks to a staff member or a virtual assistant to free your time. (3) Have your family hold you accountable. No golf if you don't follow through.

You could adopt this process for the five bad habits that you identified earlier. If we want things to change, then we must change. I've done this and it has made a big difference to me and my business. Follow through and take action.

Key Development Point

Identify and correct bad habits. Maintain and then build good habits. If we want things to change, we must change.

When I ran my small retail business I had to wear many hats – sales, distribution, finance and customer service. If you're in this position or if you're an MD or senior director, you'll have loads of stuff that needs doing. But when did you last check that all the stuff that needs doing needs doing by you? Because I bet it doesn't. I proved this hundreds of times in the past. Without realizing, we form the habit of adding more and more to our role. I've worked with people in the past where they want to control more than they need to. I've worked with people in the past who appoint senior people to do a certain job, and because they can't let go they do their own job and the job of the person they've just appointed! Because of this need their role becomes too big to manage and some of the key things that they are responsible for slip. I've seen first-hand where projects have stalled because the MD wants to input and they haven't had time to do so.

We need to keep focus on what is key, what is making the most of our strengths.

To be effective we need to keep focus on what is key, what is making the most of our strengths.

We have to build our lives and businesses around our natural abilities, the things that we do extremely well that others just can match us for. This was the main outcome when I moved out of my retail business and spent time with my wife deciding on and creating this business. Which business could I create that would enable me to be very profitable, do what I'd love to do while utilizing my key strengths? Rich Schefren in his excellent report 'Internet Business Manifesto' said that the number one reason why people aren't successful in business is because they are in the wrong business. He said that you should understand the difference between what you are interested in and what your strengths are.

A word of caution

I know that the fun card can sometimes be overplayed. I love what I do but there are parts of it that are not fun, there are things that just need to be done. They're not fun but they are essential. I get that and I'm prepared to do some things today that I don't want to do in order to have what I want to have tomorrow. Do you do that? Or do you put off the hard stuff and go for the easy or comfortable stuff that isn't a stretch. In his excellent book *A Road Less Travelled*, M. Scott Peck talks about delayed gratification. His point is that delayed gratification is a key skill that young people should be taught. This is a key skill for later in life. Doing the difficult things first, delaying the good feelings for later on rather than doing what we want to do and putting off what we need to do. My business is going to provide me with a beautiful home and pension. It provides all my food and clothes. It also pays for my holidays and our home in Valencia. If you expect your business or job to do the same for you, then isn't it worth sacrificing some time and focusing on what needs to be done? We have to commit to our businesses and get tasks done. But for the most part of your week you should be spending time on the things that you do really well, the things that you would do even if you didn't get paid for doing them. These are the things you naturally do well, you have developed the skills for and you have had training in.

How much time have you allowed yourself this week to do the things you excel at? Your happiness, income and profit levels will be directly linked to how much time you spend 'on purpose'. If your business is not where you want it to be or your sales level is not what you want it to be, check how much time you are spending on the things that you do exceptionally and the things that add value directly to your business. It is possible that things are getting in the way of you doing your best work. Once again, your business should be built around your key strengths.

For you to achieve success in your life you need to be aware of how you spend your time and on what things most of your time is taken up. I did this exercise with a client recently; they were very surprised with what we found. This is described very well in Jurgen Wolff's book *Focus*.

List the 10 tasks that take up most of your work time:

1 _____

2 _____

3 _____

4 _____

5 _____

6 _____

7 _____

8 _____

9 _____

10 _____

After you have listed the tasks, then list how much time you've spent on these tasks and work out what percentage of your total time was spent on this task. For example, if you work 40 hours a week (I know it would be nice when running a business) and 4 hours a week were spent on answering email, then that would be 10% of your weekly time.

List the three things that add the most value at work:

1 _____

2 _____

3 _____

As before, note the time spent on these tasks and the percentage or your working week.

I did this exercise recently with a client and the results were amazing. My client spent 52 hours that week in her business. Of the 52 hours, the top 10 tasks that took the most time added up to 41 hours. The three tasks that added the most value only added up to 11 hours. She was spending 80% of her time on non-productive tasks and only 20% of her time on the tasks that really added value to her business. Most of the non-productive tasks were things that she was not brilliant at and were not her strengths. The 20% of high value tasks were things that she was particularly good at; these were the things she had been trained for and was skilled in.

To help assess your starting point, this would be a good exercise for you to do. If you have a team, share it with them, reward the best performer with a Friday early finish! If you do this with your team be sure to explain why you are doing this. People need to feel engaged in the process and understand how the results will lead to more satisfaction in their role and better results for the business as a whole.

We really need to take responsibility for where we are in our businesses and our lives in general.

Finally, I'd like you to think about this for a moment: 'The reason your business is doing so well is because of you – well done! But the reason your business is only doing so well is because of you.' We really need to take responsibility for where we are in our businesses and our lives in general. A major area to take responsibility for is our habits, and remember that every bad habit needs to be replaced with a good habit.

Your habits will determine your future; what you do today will affect what you receive tomorrow. Developing your habits is not an overnight event, but over time things get amazing.

3

Your Crystal Clear Vision

At this point you have identified your bad habits and looked at how they are affecting you. More importantly, you have begun building your good habits and thought about what successful habits people you admire have. Now it's time to start building your 1-3-5 Action Plan.

What are you focusing on right now? OK, don't be clever and say 'this book, Pete'. I mean in your business or life. What is your major focus? Do you know? Is it clear? Is it getting you to where you want to be? Do you carry your current major goal around with you on a piece of card, your smartphone or tablet?

Being focused is vital. As I've already said, finding the most rewarding and profitable things to focus on is key!

Learn how to separate the majors and minors. A lot of people don't do well simply because they major in minor things.
Jim Rohn

There is a curse and many people in business have it. I call it the entrepreneurial curse. It's a curse because for people in business an active mind can mean that it's difficult to focus. Do you see loads of options? Do you notice hundreds of opportunities that other normal people just don't notice? Well, here's the curse, because of your active mind you're not focusing on the things you do brilliantly and you're not clear about exactly what you want. You have to be aware that you are being opportunistic, you need to be strategic and you need to be strategic about your crystal clear Vision. These other opportunities may seem attractive and appealing. But when you are running your small business or working in a key role within a business, you really need to be focusing on what is going to allow you to make progress in the planned direction while utilizing your key strengths. Avoid being distracted by the things that will take you away from your Vision.

Think about it now. I'm sure you can come up with a scenario where you were moving in a certain direction and then boom, something comes along that looks more attractive (usually in the short term) and you change course. After a few weeks on this revised course you realize that it is not the right course for you. You revert back to what you were doing, although some of your momentum has been lost. I'm not saying that achieving success is a straight line, it isn't, but if you can follow a plan and stay on track you can save time in reaching your goals, objectives and Vision. I'm sure you'd like to reach your Vision in 5 or 7 years instead of 10.

Back to my question at the start of this section. What are you focusing on right now?

The first component of becoming Unstoppable is Vision. Having a crystal clear Vision is the start. How clear do you see the big picture? I'm sure you've heard of the phrase 'a helicopter view'. This is what we're talking about here. I'm a very focused person but unless I'd had a crystal clear Vision of what I was going to achieve I would not have the business and life that I have right now. I find that my clients are more successful when they develop a Vision-led strategy. They also feel more confident because they know where they are heading. People talk about being pulled toward their Vision rather than having to push all of the time. Plus, when you have clarified your Vision you will find it easier to engage others in your plan. You can't be successful by yourself and the better you are at engaging others to help with your cause the easier it will be for you.

The better you are at engaging others to help with your cause the easier it will be for you.

Many business owners tell me that they have a Vision. I've read lots of corporate Visions and most if not all would be very hard to engage with. These corporate Visions tend to be about the business and often don't even mention the customer and what they are going to receive. All your business is about is delivering a result (a product or service) that your customer feels is worth more than they pay for that result. Just make sure that what you deliver has a higher value (can be perceived) than its monetary equivalent. If you do that enough times you'll be successful. Because of this I like to include some of what my clients receive in my Vision, it's as much about them as it is about me. When people tell me they have a Vision, I catch them out by asking them to read it to me. They often mumble some sentences, jump around a bit and end up saying 'something like that'. That's not good enough. It's not good enough because if you don't have a crystal clear picture of the type of life that you'd want and a crystal clear picture of the type of business that you'd want, how on earth could you create it? You could end up like the many business owners who finish each week not feeling fulfilled in their business because they are not engaged and motivated about what the big picture is and what they are in the process of creating. If you are fed up with reaching the end of the week and not feeling fulfilled in your business, do something about it.

I don't want you to end up like the thousands of people who work really hard but finish each week not feeling fulfilled. They are not fulfilled with their lives because they are not engaged and motivated about where they are heading. They don't have a clear picture of where they are heading. If you are fed up of reaching the end of the week and not feeling fulfilled with your work or your life, do something about it!

Become Unstoppable and get crystal clear about your Vision.

Going back to Gustave Eiffel and his Eiffel Tower, do you think that he had a Vision of what it was going to look like, its width and height, before they even put the spade in the ground? Of course he did. He will have had in his mind first an absolutely clear picture of what the tower was going to look like. Stephen Covey in his classic book *The 7 Habits of Highly Effective People* talks about one of the habits being begin with the end in mind. He goes on to say, 'To begin with the end in mind means to start with a clear understanding of your destination. It means to know where you're going so that you better understand where you are now and that the steps you take are always in the right direction.' When you create your Vision you're creating that picture of what success looks like to you before you even start.

I expect that you've already started and are running your business or strategic business unit right now. In order to maximize your progress and multiply your results, we're going to clarify your Vision.

Here's where the excitement starts. Your Vision is going to give you an overall focus. It's going to frame what you do every single day. It's going to pull you towards success the way gravity pulls an apple to earth. It's possible you haven't clarified what your Vision will look like. In order to help you, between you and me here's my Vision. Remember, it's my Vision and it may not resonate with you. The reason I'm showing you this is so you know what you're going to create.

Here's my Vision:

VISION

I have built a super successful coaching and speaking business that has a monthly turnover of (sales target) by (date) by utilizing my God given skills of naturally motivating and inspiring people to become focused and consistent to achieve what they want out of their lives and businesses. I have a range of products and services that enable people to make sustainable change and growth. This means that I will then be able to achieve what I would like from my life and business for my family and myself.

When you create your Vision you'll be miles ahead of the other people that don't have a clue. Just imagine you're going on holiday with your family. If you are like me you normally have more than yourself to think about. In fact, one year at our house in Spain there were nine of us and not much of a holiday for my wife and me! Let me paint an unrealistic picture for you. You arrive at your local airport. There are you, your partner, maybe the kids and possibly some grandparents. You're all together and you're all standing in front of the huge boards that show all of the flights. You look to your partner and say 'OK, its 2pm, if we get a rush on we can catch the 3pm flight to Spain or if you fancy Italy we could catch the 4.30pm. But if you really want to go to Mexico, then we'll have to sleep on the chairs and wait until 9.30am tomorrow.'

Now how funny does that sound? It sounds ridiculous doesn't it? If you were taking your family away on holiday you would have picked a destination. You would know what currency to take. If your children loved to swim you'd book a hotel with a swimming pool. If your partner loved the beach you wouldn't book a hotel 25 miles inland!

So, depending on your Vision of an excellent holiday, and if you are running a small business they can be rare to begin with, you would have certain Core Objectives and Goals to deliver that Vision. You would have to book the time off work, make sure you pack your clothes, ensure everyone has a valid passport, etc. Why is it then that when it comes to our businesses or lives in general many of us just wing it without ever stopping and deciding what a fantastic business and life looks like to us?

Your Vision is NOT going to be too corporate. I've read some company Visions and have been totally turned off. Your Vision is going to be engaging. It's going to incorporate what you do, who you do it for and what they'll get. It's going to say what you'll receive and what you'll be able to do with what you receive. It's going to clearly and succinctly describe what success means to you and WHY you want it. To achieve any lasting success WILL power is not enough, you need (and often forget) WHY power.

Your Vision for the purpose of your 1-3-5 Action Plan is going to be a succinct four to five sentence statement. It has to be short enough for you to remember it and it has to be detailed enough to describe what you're going to achieve.

Your Vision is the real starting point. Because of this we're going to get it right. I've created this 7-Step process for you to follow so that you can create a powerful, big Vision for yourself.

We think in pictures. If I asked you what your front door was like, you probably have a picture in your mind of what it looks like. You would notice the colour; maybe see the number and the handle. We're going to start with a very simple picture of what your business is going to look like. To help you and show that I've done this exercise before, I've included the actual drawing I did of what I wanted my business to look like when I began to create my Vision:

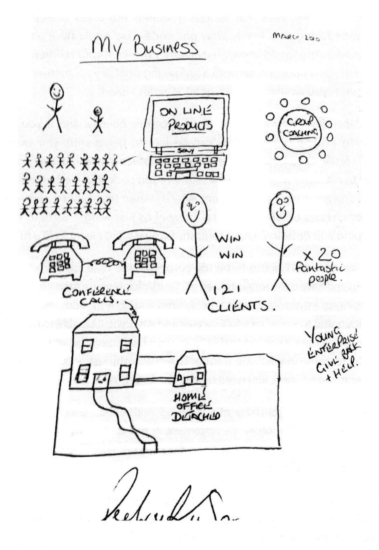

Step 1 – Create your picture.

Don't take it too seriously, we're going to make this bit fun and as easy as possible. I think you'd agree that mine doesn't demonstrate exceptional artistic flair but it worked for me. In the following space have a go at

YOUR VISION

drawing what you would like to create. Think about the different components that would make up an ideal business and structure for you.
You'll see from my picture that it involves my laptop to signify my online
coaching products. I have a picture of me presenting to audiences to
share my ideas and content to help them become more focused and
consistent. It also has a picture of a detached house and a separate office
as that is what I would love to have in the future. Again, this is what is
personal to you.

**Step 2 – Collect some photographs of the things you would
like to have in your life.**

I collected mine from magazines and catalogues. Part of one of my
client's Vision is to live in an eco-friendly house on some cliffs with a view
of the sea and free-range chickens. She has a picture of what that looks
like to her. You may love exotic holidays and have a picture of a hammock
on a private beach. Spend a little time and begin to collect photographs
of some of the things and experiences that success will enable you to
have. When you've got a good collection that shows you the life and
business that you're going to have, put them in a journal or paste them
to a white board. This is where we start to build motivational juices. We
think in pictures and this will help with our WHY power. Will power is
not enough, we need on occasion, if things get tough, to remember the
reason why we are doing things. If you are working hard and then feel
the urge to drift off in a different direction or start to tread water instead
of making progress, looking at your picture of what success means to you
can spur you on and get you back on track.

Step 3 – Describe what a perfect day looks like.

Let's say you get in from the office and you say to your partner or friend
'I've had a fantastic day today.' Describe what you did that day that made
it a fantastic day. What were you doing? Who did you spend it with? What
value were you delivering? What impact were you making on people's lives?

The outcome we're looking for here is to understand the ingredients of a successful day and record them so that we can take the steps to experience more of them. You must have had a day where you were in the groove and your workflow was great. That was you being at your best. Time probably flew by and although you felt tired at the end of the day, you knew deep inside that you had achieved some great results. Those are the days when you were on fire. It's great when you discover what you were doing and then take action to create more of them.

In the following space note some your perfect day ingredients.

_____

_____

_____

_____

_____

_____

Step 4 – Imagine what life will be like when you achieve your Vision.

How is your family going to benefit? What will you spend your leisure time doing? How will you feel when your business or career is the success it can be and you fulfil your potential? In the space provided note some of your thoughts and we'll come back to these a little later. We're building the feelings here about success so we can associate with what we will receive. This is central because if you don't know how you are going to feel and what the benefit will be to you, why will you want to work smart in your business 40 hours a week stretching yourself?

Now, this is optional, it's up to you. But I found great benefit in writing a future paced statement in the present tense about how great my life is. The idea here is that at the beginning I wanted to have something I could read regularly that would stir my emotions. I wanted something to describe clearly how great my life is because I took action on a consistent basis. This was important for me because I have high expectations for myself and I knew that some of the tasks I was going to complete to reach my goals were going to test me and shift my comfort zone. When I read my statement I reconnect emotionally and it boosts my WHY power.

Step 5 – Measure your success.

We need to come up with some areas that we can measure. In my Vision I talk about monthly sales turnover (18-odd years of retail experience mean I have to) and then an income figure. The reason I have this is because in order to have the life that I want and support my family the way I want

I'm going to need a certain level of income. Brian Tracy in his *Psychology of Achievement Programme* talks about the 'Six Elements of Success'.

These are:

1. Peace of Mind – freedom of fear, anger and guilt

2. Health and Energy – having a feeling of well-being

3. Loving Relationships – having time to spend with our loved ones

4. Financial Freedom – having enough to live on so we're not preoccupied with money

5. Worthy Goals and Ideals – we're goal-seeking mechanisms

6. Feeling of Personal Fulfilment – self-actualization according to Maslow

Looking at these six elements of success, having financial freedom is very important to me. This is why in my Vision I have a target of the income I would like to have to achieve financial freedom. It's important to note here that this is not about everyone becoming a millionaire. For some people £10,000 a year is enough; others need more than £100,000 to live the life they want. It's personal to you.

So, now start to look at a performance measure you can track against that will show you that your business or career is a success. For you this could be turnover. It could be number of clients, gross recurring income, projects delivered, or delivering a net worth value. The important thing is that numbers tell the story. You see it's not about effort. There are lots of people who work very hard, putting in the effort, but if it's not focused effort, if it's not directed towards a worthy goal, then they will not be successful. Don't finish the week and think I did OK. Finish the week and be able to say I'm further ahead, and by the end of the year I'm going to be here, which will lead to here. Let's get specific. Have a figure to focus on that means something to you. In the space provided put some of the measures that you're going to focus on that will form part of your Vision.

_____

_____

_____

_____

_____

_____

Step 6 – Get clear about the value you're going to deliver.

Here we're talking about what our target customers or clients will experience because of us. What value will they receive? In what way will they benefit? Doing this step will also help you with the rest of your marketing communications when we get to the skills part of the book.

Are you going to help people make more money? Are you going to improve people's health? Are you going to enable their business to run better? Are you going to enable them to protect their future? When you're thinking about this, keep coming back to the feature, the benefit and the value you deliver. I find that by inserting 'which means' in the sentence helps to get clarity.

Instead of just saying 'I help people to have better health' it would be much more powerful to say 'I help people to have better health, which means they can still run around and have fun with their grandchildren'.

We want to drill down to what is the value of being healthy to the sort of people you help. If you work with senior citizens in a chiropractic clinic (like one of my clients), enabling them to enjoy time with their grandchildren is a very powerful message.

For me in my Vision I talk about helping people to make massive and sustainable change so they achieve more in a week than most do in a month. They get real business growth and have the freedom to enjoy themselves. Wouldn't you want that?

In the space provided write down some of the ways in which your customers or clients receive value from you. Being able to clearly communicate the value you create for your customers and clients is important. It is also very useful in the recruitment of more of your ideal clients. You will be much further ahead when you can clearly communicate what value you create for people. It is also worth noting that many businesses don't do this very well. It is also one of the reasons why many businesses don't receive the price for their products and services they feel they are worth.

If you are struggling to come up with some of the values and benefits of what you do, then you can always ask some of your existing clients. I've found that my clients are happy to help with this. You may learn a few surprises!

_____

_____

_____

_____

_____

_____

_____

Let's recap where we are at.

We talked about how important it is to have a foundation; I used the Eiffel Tower as an example. I find that many businesses have not got a solid foundation. It's as though they are built on shifting sand. When you see a business doing well one minute and then not the next, often you could point to a shaky foundation.

For a minute, think about your life right now. If you are not reaching the goals and experiencing the results you deserve have a look at your foundation. Are you absolutely clear where you are going and how you are going to get there? Chances are that in the area you are not happy with the foundation could be stronger.

Getting into the detail

Physical training and keeping healthy are vitally important to me. When my health and fitness weren't where I wanted them to be I have to be honest and say that my foundation wasn't strong. The first thing I had to do was to create a picture of what I wanted my health to look like. I'd like to stress here that it's not about being perfect, it's about making a start and making progress. You can correct your Vision as you move along.

OK, I'm expecting that you have taken some time out and completed the six steps above. What we need to do now is to pull of all of that together and create a nice, clear, succinct four to five sentence Vision statement, like mine you've already seen. As I've previously said, this doesn't have to be perfect at this stage. All of what you have done already, including your drawing of the picture of your ideal business or collecting some pictures, is all going to be kept and used as motivational messages to remind you of where you are heading. I refer to mine when I need a little boost before completing a task that I know is going to stretch me. I find it useful to 'check in' with what I am going to achieve. But for now and for the purpose of creating your own 1-3-5 we're going to distil it down to the juicy bits.

Your Vision is going to start by describing what you do and for whom. It will then say how these people benefit and what value they experience. Next, it will say what result or measure your business will achieve, what that result will enable you to do and who will benefit from that result. It's vital here that you understand that your Vision is constructed with how your customers/clients will benefit and THEN how you will benefit.

As for a time scale to achieve your Vision, many clients like to write their Vision for 3 years out, others prefer 5 years out. That's up to you; however,

I would point out that we're going to build the successful habit of taking daily action, doing some stuff we may not want to do but stuff that needs doing. With this in mind, don't write your Vision too far out so that you think you've got years and years and don't start anything now. What we do today in the next 86,400 seconds will affect tomorrow. Finally, we must learn and practise the art of giving first in order to receive, classic reap what you sow stuff.

What we do today in the next 86,400 seconds will affect tomorrow.

! Key Development Point

It is really important to remember to write your Vision clearly as if you've already achieved it.

By this I mean don't write 'I'm going to build a successful business that supports these people to do this' but write 'I have a fantastic business that supports these people to achieve these results…'. We want to build the belief that you have already achieved it so that our subconscious mind goes to work and makes it so.

When I first did this covering the six steps above I didn't create the exact Vision that I have now. Please don't worry about it being perfect. I really want you to do this as I know it will make a massive difference to your life and business. Just start writing – go on, do it now!

Step 7.

In the following space write down your own first draft of your business/ life Vision.

_____

_____

_____

_____

_____

_____

_____

_____

_____

_____

Brilliant! I bet it feels good to have a simple statement that you can remember that describes what your life and business are going to be like. Now, when you are ready to develop it further you'll find it beneficial to build some real emotional connection to it. You can put some words in that you would use to make it emotionally charged. Also, you'll find it better to write it like you can really believe it's possible. We want to feel amazing when we read it and imagine our life and business are like that. When you develop yours to become what Napoleon Hill calls 'a burning desire' in _Think and Grow Rich_, you'll accelerate towards it much more effectively.

When I read mine, at least every Monday morning when I start the week, the hairs on the back of my neck stand up. I sit at my desk and slide open the right-hand drawer. I have my 1-3-5 in a clear wallet and read it and reconnect. Just imagine for a moment what it is going to be like for you when you get to the office or somewhere comfortable, get out your 1-3-5, read your Vision and the hairs on the back of your neck stand up. Isn't that going to be a fantastic way for you to start your week? Can you imagine how much more you will achieve when you start your week really motivated and have your Vision at the centre of what you do?

Here's what Chris Gillie, MD from Heritage Accountancy, said after he developed his Vision with the rest of his senior team:

Every day having our company vision makes me more engaged and focused and also highlights that it isn't something that can be achieved overnight but with small steps (goals) to begin with eventually turning into a sprint. Small steps in the right direction are a far cry from previously being in a constant fire fight.

 Key Development Point

Clarify and then read your Vision weekly, you need to connect with it and keep it front of mind. This is going to drive all of your actions.

4

Your 3 Core Objectives

Congratulations, you've taken action on the first stage of creating the life and business you want and you've taken the first step in creating your own personal 1-3-5 Action Plan. You can feel good for a few minutes... but now it's back to work as the next stage needs to be created!

You now have your Vision. You've created a simple, succinct statement of what success looks like to you. Your Vision is your grand picture; it's a total helicopter view of your business with a personal element that will be about 3–5 years out. Now is the time to chunk it down.

The overall purpose of creating your 1-3-5 Action Plan is so that you have a proven plan that enables you to take focused action on a consistent basis so that you become exceptional and ultimately Unstoppable. If you just leave it at the Vision stage it would be incomplete. Yes, you will be feeling good with your Vision but in order for you to truly achieve it, you have to take some action. Action is the essential ingredient in life; only what you think about, talk about and then do something about

Having a picture of what you want but not having a plan of how it's going to happen can be very frustrating.

will actually come about. In fact it's fair to say that having a picture of what you want but not having a plan of how it's going to happen can be very frustrating.

With your Vision being so grand you'll be wondering where to start. This is where your 3 Core Objectives come in – chunking down your Vision to make it more achievable. You couldn't eat an elephant in one go, you would have to chunk it down; this is what we're going to do here. We're going to focus here on the things that are absolutely core to you achieving your Vision. If something is not absolutely core, then it is simply nice-to-have not a must-have.

When I got to this stage I found it quite challenging. I have an active mind and because of that there are loads of things I could focus on. Have you ever started something and then gone off in a different direction? Have you ever chased a bright blue butterfly? By this I mean be working on an important project and then when you get to a tough bit or something pops up on your laptop (like email, YouTube, Twitter or Facebook) you move off in that area because it looks more interesting. If you have done this before, then setting your 3 Core Objectives is going to be perfect for you.

You may be wondering why we have 3 Core Objectives. The reason we have 3 is because if you are like most of the business professionals I support and present to, you probably have more to do than you have time to do it. You probably have a task list that never gets complete and there are often things carried over to the next day or even the next week. One of the main reasons for this is that

If something is not absolutely core, then it is simply nice-to-have not a must-have.

you are focusing on too many things. Your focus is being spread too thinly and your efforts are being diluted to the point where in some weeks you begin to wonder what impact you have had. You will be relieved to learn that many people in business have had weeks where they are really busy doing stuff but often get to the end of the week and wonder where the time has gone and question what impact they have had. I have met many people in business who have had busy weeks but have not actually achieved anything. You are going to be in the minority who focus on making progress and feel good about the progress you make.

Having 3 Core Objectives will ensure that you cover the main objectives that are needed to achieve your Vision, and this is where you are going to direct your attention and focus. Everything we do from now on has the purpose of enabling you to achieve your Vision in an effective way as quickly and efficiently as possible. Now I'm not saying fast here. Achieving anything notable is going to take time. What I am saying is that many people overestimate what they can achieve in a day or a week and underestimate what they can achieve in 90 days or even a year.

Achieving anything notable is going to take time.

Paul Callaghan from Leighton Group (which is a Sunderland, UK-based, successful group of five independent companies) said:

> *Good leaders have to understand what their objectives are and they've got to carry people along with them.*

You're going to be in a great place when you know the 3 Core Objectives that are central to your success. There's a feeling of confidence you'll experience when you know you're on track. Being able to share these with your support team and possibly the people in your business will help you become aligned. Let's move ahead here in time. When we have completed this next part and you have your 3 Core Objectives that are central to completing your Vision, you will have the three main areas that you are going to focus on. If you undertake a task that doesn't directly contribute to one or all of your Core Objectives, then you need to question why you are doing that task. Because your 3 Core Objectives are central to the completion of your Vision, the majority of your time should be spent on achieving them, not being distracted by other less important tasks and activities.

Creating your 3 Core Objectives

Starting with Core Objective 1, you need to ask yourself: what is the first thing that absolutely needs to be in place for you to reach your Vision? Remember, these Core Objectives are central.

Here are some examples to get you going. Let's say you ran an accountancy business, your Core Objective 1 could be to do with the level of your gross recurring income. So, if you want your small practice to achieve £1m of turnover then a critical factor could be how many clients you have that pay you every year for completing their accounts. Depending on your mix of clients and the rate at which they pay you, that will give you a gross recurring income.

If you were a chiropractor, then the number of clients on a particular payment plan again contributing to turnover would be a good Core Objective.

A client I worked with recently chose a Core Objective around the value delivered to his shareholders so they would continue to invest in his business and allow him to continue to develop his business.

If you were a training or coaching professional, Core Objective 1 may be how much income you want from a particular income stream or product line in a 12-month period.

I personally like Core Objectives of this nature because they emphasize that you are only going to achieve Core Objective 1 by helping people to do or have something before they pay you. Whatever business you are in, you need people. That may be people to support you, people you support, or people you identify as paying clients.

My Core Objective 1 is related to my passive income from my online coaching and development programmes. The more people I can reach, the more people I can have an impact on. Delivering content online enables me to reach far more people around the globe and at the same time is a great way to leverage my time.

 Key Development Point

Before you dash off and write your Core Objective 1, I want to stress the three main things that your objectives need to be:

1. They must be core.

2. They must be specific.

3. They must be written like you've achieved them.

Vague objectives produce vague results. Don't say 'I do well and I have lots of customers' or 'my sales performance is big'. Say 'I have £600k of recurring income each year from my 300 core clients'.

The more specific you can be, the easier it will become when we reach the 5 Goal setting stage.

In the following space write down your Core Objective 1:

_____

_____

_____

_____

_____

_____

_____

_____

Now we move on to Core Objective 2. I find that with Core Objective 2 many businesses choose to focus on process and system. Thinking about your Vision you've created, what process and system would need to be in place? When you look at the success of McDonald's (whether you like the food or not) it is clear that their 'system' has played a massive part. They have systems for everything. They have a system for building the restaurant, recruiting staff and for management development. But the system that Ray Kroc (who joined McDonald's in 1954 and built it into the most successful fast food operation in the world) was so impressed with was the simple system of how they produced their product in an efficient way, i.e. a burger. That system has enabled them to grow massively, operate all over the world and be what Michael E. Gerber in his excellent book *The E-Myth* calls the best small business in the world.

So looking critically at your business Core Objective 2 could be about having a proven delivery system that enables you to grow your business and achieve your Vision. You could set the objective of developing an excellent marketing or lead generation system that enables you to reach your sales target. Thinking ahead (the future is where more of our thinking needs to be), if you had an excellent marketing plan that you executed well that delivered a stream of clients (a certain number), would that be good? Would that be essential to you developing the life and business that you want? If it would, then that could be the basis of your Core Objective 2.

If you are a manufacturing or retail business your Core Objective 2 could be about how you deliver your product. It would be the development of a system or process manual that enables you to achieve a sustainable competitive advantage. You could create a more profitable way of delivering your product, which also benefits your customers.

Many people I work with in workshops set their Core Objective 2 as a team development one in relation to their people and having a high performance team. That also may work for you.

My Core Objective 2 is centred on my face-to-face 121 and team coaching programmes, as for me to reach my Vision I need to work with a certain number of professional teams and have a certain number of 121 clients. I would find it impossible to feel fulfilled in my business if I wasn't working with people on a personal basis. That works for me but it may be different for you.

I'm giving you these examples to get you thinking. If you are part of a team you could come up with your Core Objectives as a group exercise. I've done this before with clients and it can work well when everyone is on side.

In the following space write down your Core Objective 2:

_____

_____

_____

_____

_____

_____

_____

Core Objective 3 is your final objective. When you become super successful, the journey there can be as rewarding as the outcome itself, well nearly! It has been said that success is not what you get, it is about who you become. Thinking totally out of the box, this objective could be to do with the person you need to be to achieve the success and the Vision you have set. You may have to develop some brilliant new habits (it's always about habits). You may have to acquire new skills. You may have to make far better use of your time. If this is the case, what evidence would you see or hear that would tell you that you have become exceptional?

Alternatively, your team may be spot on and your Core Objective 3 is related to a new product that will enable you to reach a new market, attract a new customer base and move into an area that is new but very profitable. It's possible that your Vision is about reaching and having an impact on many people, far more that you impact on today. If that is the case, having a Core Objective to focus on in that area could be critical.

I was working with a group of chief executives recently and one of the guys decided that for his 1-3-5 Action Plan his 3 Core Objectives were going to be Core Objective 1 personal, Core Objective 2 business and Core Objective 3 spiritual. He felt that for him to make the most of himself and live the life that he wanted, these were absolutely core.

My Core Objective 3 is centred on the speaking and presenting part of my business. In order for me to reach and support the number of people I want to I have to speak to large audiences. Plus, I absolutely love speaking and for me it's about making the best use of my key strength (we'll get to that later on). So, my last objective is describing the result I'm going to achieve by developing that side of my business.

In the following space write down your Core Objective 3:

_____

_____

_____

_____

_____

_____

_____

_____

Excellent, we're really making progress now. You must be feeling pleased with yourself; that's stage 2 of the 1-3-5 Action Plan foundation complete. Looking back at your 3 Core Objectives, do you feel that they are absolutely core? Be careful your Core Objectives are not just simple goals. They are meant to stretch you and not be something you could achieve with your eyes shut.

Here are my 3 Core Objectives that are the three central parts to my business, which must be achieved in order for me to realize my Vision and reach and impact on the number of people I want to support:

Core Objective 1	Core Objective 2	Core Objective 3
I have built a range of online success programmes to provide a passive income of (fig) a month or more by (date)	I have built and expanded my group and 1 2 1 coaching programmes to provide a monthly turnover of (fig) or more by (date) and have at least X IMA Team clients	I have built and developed my speaking business to provide a monthly turnover of (fig) or more by (date)

Now look back over the 3 Core Objectives you have just created and check that each of these is absolutely essential in enabling you to achieve your Vision.

One last thing to note is that your Core Objectives need to be tight. By that I mean they are brief enough for you to remember. Keep them brief and not long winded. Remember that the overriding premise of your 1-3-5 Action Plan is that you will use it.

❗ Key Development Point

Keeping your Core Objectives as tight as possible means that you can read your 1-3-5 Action Plan in minutes, you'll then be able to get on with job of making it happen. Action is essential!

Let's recap where we're at.

You now have your Vision written out like you have achieved it and it's packed with emotion that you are connected to. When you read it the hairs on the back of your neck stand up and it's going to put you in an exceptional state on a Monday morning when you read it. It's something to be proud of and a thing of beauty.

You have also created your 3 Core Objectives. You are now going to do a quick recheck and make sure that the Core Objectives you have set are absolutely core, are specific and are written like you have achieved them. Be honest, do they really need to be in place for you to achieve your Vision?

Great, you now have your 3 Core Objectives that are the areas that you are going to direct your focus on a monthly basis. If you find yourself doing something that will not lead to the completion of one of your 3 Core Objectives, then question why you are doing it. This is a critical step in ensuring that you stay on track. Remember my comment regarding bright blue butterflies? That's not you, you're on purpose, you're focused on achieving your Vision and you're now focused on the successful completion of your 3 Core Objectives.

If you have a good sense of humour, this will make you laugh. When I get asked to work with someone on a project that is not going to help me achieve one of my Core Objectives or if someone wants a meeting with me and I really don't have the time, I now 'blame' my Core Objectives. It's amazing the response I get when I respectfully reply 'I'd help you with that project if I could but my Core Objectives won't allow it, I must stay on task.' It's only a bit of fun but it still amuses me how many people go 'er, OK, Pete, I understand'.

But on a serious note, many people start things and don't finish them. They drift off in a different direction. One of the major reasons for this is that they don't know what they should be working on and why they should be working on it – be different! Being consistent is vital for you to make the most of yourself and live the life that you want and deserve. A great quote that springs to mind now is from Andrew Carnegie who in 1901 sold his steel business for $401m; he said:

As I get older I pay less attention to what people say; I just watch what they do.

It is worth reading that a couple of times. When I first read it I pledged that I was going to be one of those people who say they're going to do something and then do it. Only what we think about, talk about and then DO something about will actually come about. It's OK if in the past you were one of the people who said they **Being consistent is vital** would do more than they actually did. From now on **for you to make the most** when you say you are going to do something, take **of yourself and live the** action to do it! The reason we are creating 3 Core **life that you want and** Objectives is so that you have the key areas in your **deserve.** business or life to focus on.

So with your 3 Core Objectives you must FOCUS, FOCUS, FOCUS!

Your Core Objectives can only be achieved if the actions around these activities can be monitored. As Peter Drucker, the management guru, said:

Basic management rules apply – what gets measured gets managed.

You've got to get good at measuring. You want to grow sales, measure sales, you want to grow margin, measure margin, and you want to grow profit, measure profit. You want to grow your happiness, and then find a way to measure your happiness! Find a way to measure your progress with the completion of your 3 Core Objectives and make sure they are set for the same time frame as your Vision.

Look at your life and business now. Be honest with yourself – what are you measuring? Do you have any specific measures in place? You can measure your diet, your fitness, your happiness, your wealth, anything. If you want something to improve, you have to measure it. When I was a company sales manager I had 12 KPIs (key performance indicators) covering a whole range of things. At the time I admit that I thought this was a little excessive. Looking back I realize that I was aware of how my business was performing in all key areas; I was measuring everything. Now, you may not want to set yourself 12 KPIs but you really should be measuring the key results that will let you know you're on track and making progress. Plus, when you start to make progress with it you'll be motivated to do more. Because one of my Core Objectives is to achieve a certain result with my 121, group and team coaching clients I have a marketing plan that describes the marketing activities that I plan to do. On that A4 sheet I track and measure various things, some of which are the number of Twitter followers I have, how many people I have on my master emailing list and the number of blogs I do. When I'm reaching these targets and I can see progress is being made (no matter how small), I'm motivated to be consistent and stick with it. As an added bonus, if my measurement shows that I'm not making the progress that I thought I would I can quickly amend what I'm doing and then hopefully through measurement see an improved result. So you've got to get good at measuring!

Part of my weekly reading of my 1-3-5 Action Plan is looking at my 3 Core Objectives and deciding on which Core Objective I am currently focusing on. I decide which is the one that needs to be acted on at that time. As I'm writing this, my current major focus is Core Objective 3. I'm really focusing on the tasks that will lead to the goals that need to be achieved in order to achieve that Core Objective. It's about having all of your activities aligned. I look at where I am and decide what would be a good result each week.

 Key Question

Do you always have a weekly outcome?

Remember that it's all about progress not perfection.

Remember that it's all about progress not perfection. Tom Peters posted recently to Twitter that in the 1980s it was 'ready, aim, fire'; in the 1990s it was 'ready, fire, aim'; and now, he said, it is 'fire, fire, fire'.

When you've set your 3 Core Objectives, keep focused on taking action to achieve them, keep making progress. I'm sure there were times, especially in the latter stages of my Triathlon, when I didn't look all that comfortable and let's be honest I wasn't moving with finesse. On occasion I've felt like Rudolf Nureyev wearing ASICS running shoes; however, at the end of my Triathlon that was not the case. The key is that I had to keep moving and achieving each Core Objective. It clearly wasn't enough to have a great bike section and smash my target time if I wasn't able to achieve Core Objective 3, which was to stand on the finishing line in one piece by 7.30pm.

You have to be looking in the right place when you're measuring and monitoring the performance of your Core Objectives. This brings us to the final and equally critical stage of your 1-3-5 Action Plan, your 5 action orientated Goals for each of your 3 Core Objectives. This is an exciting stage where we get into the detail. Here is where you start to look at what is going to enable you to keep focused on a daily basis and make the very best of your 86,400 seconds every day. Those days that you may have had where you are really busy but not effective will be a distant memory!

Key Development Point

If what you are doing isn't contributing to one of your 3 Core Objectives, question whether you should be doing it.

5

Your 5 Goals

One of the major reasons why people don't get to where they want to be is because they can't see a route. In fact, whenever you get lost in the car it's because you lose the signposts and are not sure which way to go. I remember being lost recently (why is it that men don't like to ask for directions?) and then I saw a signpost and thought 'get in' – I immediately felt better and happier to be on track again. Let's replicate that feeling with your business and life progress. Let's design some signposts so you know where you're going and you can measure the inevitable progress you'll soon be making. Wouldn't that be a good thing? This is why it is crucial to set goals.

This is the critical stage where we start to nail down what needs to be done every day that will enable you to reach and achieve your magnificent Vision. Please understand that when I say 'your magnificent Vision' I'm referring to what that means to you. My Vision probably would not excite you and yours may not excite me. Just make sure that your Vision excites you!

The three main things your goals need to be are:

1. Stepping stones

2. Action orientated

3. Outcome focused

Let's look at these in a little more detail.

1. Stepping stones

First, your goals should be stepping stones. If you were to look back earlier at my Ultra Endurance Triathlon 1-3-5 Action Plan you'll see that my goals were stepping stones to achieving that particular Core Objective. What I mean by this is I want you to realize that this Unstoppable system and specifically at this stage your foundation 1-3-5 Action Plan is a process. Ultimately, I've created the process so you can simply build a plan of what you are you going to do, where you are going to focus and how you are going to be consistent in order for you to build the life and business that you want. So my idea of your goals being stepping stones is to emphasize that the only reason you have goals is to make progress. Your goals are also to going to be dynamic. By this I mean that you will replace them as you achieve them. When I achieve one of my goals in my 1-3-5 Action Plan I highlight it in bold italics so that I know I've achieved it and feel a little satisfaction for a short while. I then replace it with another goal to focus on, always making progress.

Thinking back to when I did my Triathlon, when I was on the bike I had goals around the amount of food I ate, the fluid I drank, the pace I maintained, the heart rate I held and the perceived feeling of effort. By focusing on these for 7 hours meant that when I reached the marathon run stage at about 3.15pm in the afternoon I had enough energy to finish the event. If I hadn't taken on enough food (the bike is where you do the majority of your fuelling) I'd have ran out of energy and not finished the event. If I'd raced too hard and my heart rate was over 160 I'd have burned out and not finished the event. The little goals that I set along the way had the sole purpose of enabling me to make progress (fairly slow at times to be honest) and get me to my Vision of finishing the event inside 14 hours. In my business I have goals that are stepping stones to achieving each of my business Core Objectives.

Your goals are going to become benchmarks, if you like, that will enable you to step onto something else. By making a little progress, bit by bit, over time you will consistently get to where you want to be.

Key Development Point

When you are setting your goals make sure that they are a bit of a stretch for you. You want to believe that they are achievable but these stepping stones need to get you to shift your comfort zone a bit.

2. Action orientated

Next, your goals are going to be action orientated. What I mean by this is that I've come across people and they set goals that don't really require any action to complete them. We're going to set your goals so that you've absolutely got to take some action in order to achieve them. Remember: thinking is good, talking is better, action is best.

Action is the essential ingredient in life; only what we think about, talk about and then do something about will actually come about. It is certainly the people who 'do' who succeed. Your goals are going to motivate you to develop the 'action habit'. You're going to become the person who gets on with taking action to get a result. I don't want you to just set goals, I want you to achieve your goals. You're not going to just be a talker. Think back briefly to the Andrew Carnegie quote earlier.

As I get older I pay less attention to what people say, I just watch what they do.

I bet you love taking action. I bet you feel fantastic when you take action. I realized a while ago that when I looked at my life and business and found I wasn't getting the result that I wanted it was because I'd lost focus and stopped taking action. Recently, I wanted to build a better level of all-round strength. Triathletes are more balanced with strength than pure cyclists and runners but we're still heavily biased towards leg strength. I wanted to do something to correct this and began with some simple press-ups. I had a goal and began doing press-ups. I don't mind sharing how hard I found them at first; 10 was a real struggle (when did you last try doing some press-ups?). But I had a goal and took action consistently, and in what seemed like no time at all I could comfortably do 40. Now, if I'd stopped when it got hard or if I hadn't developed the 'action habit' I would not have reached 40, my goal. It's exactly the same with your business. I've seen clients achieve so much when they have set action orientated goals. One client increased their client base by 97% in 12 months by setting goals. Another client increased their monthly sales level by 54%. Now it is time for you to set 5 action orientated Goals for each of your 3 Core Objectives. Make sure they are stepping stones to lead to something bigger; develop the action habit and you'll make an amazing amount of progress.

Jumping ahead slightly here, action cures procrastination too. If you want to prove this, try this. Next time you're lying in bed and the alarm goes off you may think, I don't want to get up I'll just lie here. If you put off getting up at that point in what Dr Tom Barratt calls your CMD, your critical moment of decision, take action, jump out of bed, throw on some clothes and see what happens. By taking action you've solved your procrastination and you're on your way. I often use the self-starter 'do it now'. When I'm thinking about working on my business and an idea pops into my head I do something with it there and then. It's amazing how much you can get done when you use the self-starter 'do it now'. It's simple but it works.

In a short while you'll have your 5 Goals for each Core Objective and you'll be taking action all the time!

3. Outcome focused

Finally, your goals will also be outcome focused. When setting goals some people don't have a clear outcome in mind, they're fairly vague. I've heard people say their goal is to 'lose some weight' or 'get more sales'. If they created a clearer outcome such as 'I want to weigh 79 kg by 15 August because I'm racing on 1 September', the chance of them staying on track and achieving their outcome would be greater. If they said 'I want to grow my business by 10% this year and reach £300,000 by 31 December', again they would find it easier to stay on track and decide what tasks need to be undertaken to achieve that outcome. One of my leg strength goals in my Triathlon 1-3-5 Action Plan wasn't to become stronger but to be able to leg press 180 kg. My outcome was clear, can I leg press 180 kg or not?

I love the Bourne films. There's a scene in the third film where Nicki says that 'they don't make mistakes, they don't do random, there's always an outcome'. Now, I'm not suggesting you go off and become a highly trained assassin for the US government, but you see the point. If you are going to make the very best of yourself, one of the things you need to do is to ensure that you always have an outcome in mind. This is why your 5 Goals for each Core Objective are going to be outcome focused. **Ensure that you always have an outcome in mind.**

Keep your goals in the right perspective

I'd like to make a real point here. The goals you set for yourself in your 1-3-5 Action Plan are there to motivate and inspire you. They are there to keep you engaged with your Vision. They are there so that you know what you should be spending your time doing. They are there so that you can feel good about the progress you are making. Your goals are not to kick you or make you feel bad about yourself. Don't set goals that make you feel at the outset 'I'll never achieve that'. Set goals that make you say 'if I really focus and work to the level I'm capable of, I know with a bit of effort I can reach that goal'. This is key because if you've ever been in an appraisal where your line manager has set a goal for you, you'll know what I mean. They set a goal and you think no chance. You're not engaged in the process and before you even start you think 'it's not going to happen'. If you've always had productive, effective appraisals with an excellent line manager you may not have experienced this. For many this is not the case. This is why here these are your goals to reach your Core Objectives so that you can achieve your Vision!

Your goals are not to kick you or make you feel bad about yourself.

Key Development Point

Your goals are to motivate you to keep taking action and fulfil your potential.

As before, when you set your 3 Core Objectives you may not get this stage right first time. This is fine, it is important that you start the process and focus on making progress. As long as you're making progress you can't fail; you only fail when stop or give up.

Some of the goals you set here will be challenging, but that is the idea. You will grow as you achieve them. Your 1-3-5 Action Plan is about you developing into the person you really are and the person you're capable of becoming. That is what success is about. You will be surprised by how easy it is when you just start doing the things that you need to do consistently to get to where you want to be.

Some of the goals you set here will be challenging, but that is the idea.

Now at this stage you may be thinking why your 1-3-5 Action Plan is going to be a 1-3-5 Action and not a 1-3-10. I created my 1-3-5 Action Plan because I wanted to think of only the really key things I'd have to achieve to achieve my Core Objectives. Plus, in business I've seen people being really busy, focusing on loads of stuff and not making any real progress. It's difficult to focus on 30 different things and when I ask people what they are working on they can give me a list as long as their arm.

The reason we have 5 Goals is so that you focus on the things right now that will enable you to make some progress. For this reason the goals in your 1-3-5 Action Plan will be dynamic. They will change frequently depending on the progress you make. So, if one of your goals for Core Objective 1 was to build an email list to 1000 people who get what you do and who could become prospects in 6 months' time, you can update that when you achieve that goal. There will be tasks sitting behind achieving that goal that you must take action on. It works for me to focus on particular goals at particular times. I set time aside in my diary to specifically work on certain goals. When I have achieved that goal I move onto the next one, each goal leads to something else. Here you are focusing on which 5 Goals are going to enable you to reach each Core Objective.

> **! Key Development Point**
>
> Beware of Action Apathy; as we get older Action Apathy can creep in and your action taking begins to slow down and eventually stops altogether.

I'll give you three examples. With exercise it's all too easy for weekly games of squash to be replaced by occasionally walking the dog and then eventually walking to the car (some people even walk into the car in their garage and then drive to their parking space right at their office). As we achieve our financial goals we become less target driven until necessity comes through the door and we become very focused. Finally, in the early days of love and lust the goals orientated action was all too obvious. But as time passes partners become less goal orientated and this often leads to a lack of, well, action! Make sure this doesn't happen to you.

It's not enough for you to just set your 5 Goals for each Core Objective. It's vital you take action to achieve those goals; don't be a goal setter, be a goal achiever.

When you think about your goals you want your attention and focus to be directed to what will make you progress. Because of this you don't want to give yourself too much to focus on. Fifteen goals are enough at one time. Also, when I've received feedback from my clients they tell me that because their 1-3-5 Action Plan fits onto a single page they are more likely to use it regularly. We know that what we focus on magnifies, so if you've got your 1-3-5 Action Plan with you close at hand and you focus on it, then the results you experience will magnify and multiply.

Goals are how to get everything you want – faster than you ever thought possible.
Brian Tracy

Your goal checklist

So, let's begin. Here's some bullet points for you to consider when you are setting your 5 Goals for each Core Objective:

- What do you want to achieve with your goal?
  Here you have your Vision that you created earlier. This is a description of what you really want. What goal could you set that will lead to making progress towards your Core Objective?

- Spend a little time just thinking about how you will be able to achieve your goal, be positive
  Belief is critical, that is why your goals are going to be a stretch but you will still believe that you can achieve them. Napoleon Hill said 'what the mind can conceive and believe it can achieve'.

- Write your goal in your 1-3-5 Action Plan template
  Many people keep their goals in their head; they are more real when you write them down.

- What is your current position in relation to your goal?
  When I set my goals for my Triathlon and one of them was to swim 4000 m in under 1.5 hours I had to know where I was to begin.

- Determine why you must achieve your goal
  Part of the process I shared earlier about creating your Vision was about building your WHY power; you need to determine why you want it.

- Set a date for goal completion
  This is key because if you don't have a deadline, then you'll drift. This is especially the case if you are a business owner without a boss as there is no one to hold your feet to the fire.

● What are the obstacles that may get in the way?
  This step is often overlooked. It's not about being negative; it's about being aware of what might happen so that you can plan a way around it.

● Is there additional knowledge and skills you need?
  You may have to upgrade your skills in order to achieve your goal; thinking about it enables you to get prepared.

● Is there someone who can help you achieve your goal?
  No one became hugely successful by themselves. In Part Four we carry out people review for the year ahead.

● Review your goals continually
  This is why you followed the process in creating your Vision and specifically collected some pictures of what you'll get so that you stay engaged. Plus, this is why I check my 1-3-5 Action Plan every week.

● Be consistent
  Being focused and consistent will be the key to your success. It's always too soon to give up. This is why we built the feeling of what we'll get when we achieve our Goals, Core Objectives and our Vision. It will keep us motivated to keep taking focused action. It's far easier to be consistent when you have a clear picture of your Vision and destination.

First, look at your Core Objective 1.

This is where making sure your Core Objectives are core, specific and written like you've achieved them will help. Think about what goals need to reach your Core Objective 1. One client I had decided that their Core Objective 1 was to be in relation to their own personal effectiveness. The outcome for them was what result they could achieve within a certain working time frame, which was less than they currently worked. Their goals for this Core Objective were about time management, using time blocks to focus on certain tasks. They also had goals around learning to delegate better with their team so that the team delivered what they were supposed to and allowed my client to work on what they should be working on. For them it was all about one important aspect: focus on return on energy. What return will you get for each 59-minute segment of time?

What return will you get for each 59-minute segment of time?

Think about your Core Objective 1. What are the five stepping stone goals you can set so that by achieving them you are progressing towards completing your objective?

If you remember, my Core Objective 1 was about building an online passive coaching income. The goals I have may be to do with building a range of online programmes at various price points. It may be setting up a membership-based website to house the programmes. It may be to do with setting up joint venture relationships with people who also serve my target audience to showcase a free introduction product to demonstrate value. If you struggle to get going with your first Core Objective think for a moment that you've achieved it. What did you have to do to achieve it? Just brainstorm some of those things that you would have had to do. From those answers you'll be able to set 5 Goals.

In the following space make a start and write down your 5 Goals for Core Objective 1. Remember, they need to be stepping stones, action orientated and outcome focused. At this stage, which may be your first attempt at building an Action Plan, your goals do not have to be perfect, the key is to get started; think about baby steps to begin with.

_____

_____

_____

_____

_____

_____

_____

_____

We'll do the same now for Core Objective 2. Another client I supported decided that their Core Objective 2 was going to be around developing a systems manual so that their offering could be easily duplicated without my client being present. Their idea was one of leverage and growth. As a result, their 5 Goals were centred on documenting the process, recording the process, producing the system manual and then testing the system and tweaking it. My Core Objective 2 was around my face-to-face coaching. I want to work with so many professional teams in a particular year. When setting my goals I had to think hard about what goals would enable me to reach those teams. My goals then became easier because I had a specific objective. I wrote things like, building five connector relationships, having an email list of suspects that I could build a relationship with, developing a range of free resources to demonstrate expert status, setting up a system-ized referral process. Largely, these goals were about the marketing steps I could take to make progress towards achieving my Core Objective 2.

In the following space write down your 5 Goals for Core Objective 2.

_____

_____

_____

_____

_____

_____

_____

_____

_____

We're nearly done and have only Core Objective 3 to do. Many people I've come across are working very hard and long hours in their business. One guy in particular wanted to have his Core Objective 3 to be solely about his work/life blend. The outcome of the objective was in relation to how much time he worked and how much time he took off to spend with his wife and family. His goals were centred on spending 1 day per month with his wife trying a new activity such as clay pigeon shooting, hot air ballooning or archery. His other goals were about his own rejuvenation time and physical training time. He knew that if he hit these goals he would achieve the Core Objective of having the ideal life blend for him. My Core Objective 3 is about the speaking and presenting side of my business. I have an objective to reach a certain level of turnover and speak a certain number of times in a year. Again, in order for this to be reached, what goals could I set? My goals are centred on the development and practice of my keynote presentation so that I become world class. I have goals around the number of showcases where I speak for no fee to ideal target audiences. I have to produce speaking marketing materials such as a one-page info sheet or a showreel of me speaking to an audience. When I achieve each of these goals I make progress towards my Core Objective. Keep thinking this is about progress. What goals can you set so that you are motivated to keep taking action? You have to be consistent with your effort. It's sending that email, writing that letter, making that phone call and even possibly having that difficult conversation. Keep at it and reward yourself for each milestone you reach. Remember to look back at how far you have come.

In the following space write down your 5 Goals for Core Objective 3.

_____

_____

_____

_____

_____

_____

_____

_____

_____

Time for a quick recap. You've identified and written down your 15 Goals. You have made sure that these are stepping stones, action orientated and outcome focused. Your goals are what you are going to focus on on a daily basis. Your goals are going to be the way you are going to maximize every single day so that you are working effectively and making progress. Make every day count, do something to work on your goals! Your goals are critical to your building momentum and achieving the life and business that you desire. Because your goals are so critical I suggest that you write out one of your goals every day for 30 days. Pick one that you really would love to achieve. I want you to get absolutely clear about what you are going to focus on daily. You see, most people don't have any goals, and in order for you to make the most use of your goals and to reward you for doing the work in the first place and setting them, you're going to constantly focus on them. Earlier I shared how important it is for you to control your thoughts. A great way to make progress is to keep your goals in your mind and write them out, imagining you've achieved them; make your goals what you are thinking about.

Make every day count, do something to work on your goals!

Here's where the magic really begins to happen.

- You have your crystal clear Vision of what you're going to achieve.

- You have your 3 Core Objectives that are absolutely central to the successful achievement of your Vision that will keep you motivated and focused on a monthly basis.

- You have your 5 action orientated Goals for each of your 3 Core Objectives so that you maintain daily focus and motivation.

What we're going to do now is pull the whole together and create a thing of beauty. You're going to create your own world class 1-3-5 Action Plan.

Here's the template we're going to use, the massively powerful 1-3-5 Action Plan foundation for the Unstoppable system.

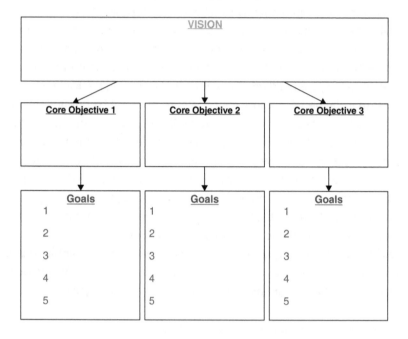

If you would like a blank template to download so that you can complete your 1-3-5 Action Plan and print it out, go to www.petewilkinson .com/1-3-5template.

Here's an idea

I hope that you can see how powerful the 1-3-5 Action Plan foundation is. I recently worked with a professional team and the chief executive was very impressed with and instantly said how he could set a 1-3-5 Action Plan for his whole business. He then took it a stage further and developed a 1-3-5 for each department that fed into the central 1-3-5. After that he decided to create a 1-3-5 for his polar expedition. You see, once you are confident that you have your 1-3-5 Action Plan complete for your business, you can use it for all sorts of projects. One client even developed a 1-3-5 for Christmas! They work very hard in their business and wanted to really enjoy their time off. With this in mind they created a simple Vision of what a good Christmas was and then 3 Core Objectives to make it happen. Their goals were around little stretches to achieve their Core Objectives. So, if you are thinking of renovating your house, having a fantastic once-in-a-lifetime family holiday or launching a new product or division in your business, you can use the 1-3-5 Action Plan to keep you on track and achieve success.

Making your foundation work

In the excellent book *Psycho-Cybernetics* by Maxwell Maltz there's a chapter entitled 'Acquiring the habit of happiness'. In this chapter, the author states that man is a goal-striving being and he goes on to say 'he is functioning naturally and normally when he is orientated toward some positive goal and striving toward some desirable goal. Happiness is a symptom of normal, natural functioning and when man is functioning as a goal-striver, he tends to feel fairly happy regardless of circumstances.'

I agree fully with this and have found in the past that when clients come to me and they are not performing well or feel a little lost it is because they have not set specific enough goals and don't have a clear picture of the outcome they would like. Have you found this with yourself?

When we set goals that are results focused and we concentrate our efforts on achieving that goal, we get into flow. We are motivated by the target that we have set. I believe that we should pursue our goals aggressively. When I'm training for a challenging endurance event I have been known to talk aggressively to myself when I get in the zone – I keep getting feedback from my wife! We should not be passive about what we want to have happen as long as what we want to have happen does not cost or negatively impact other people.

We should not be passive about what we want to have happen.

If you have observed someone who acts like they have lost, chances are they have lost their aggressive attitude towards achieving a goal. When your goals excite you and engage you then you are on a mission and nothing will be allowed to get in the way. This is the point when you get momentum on your side. I've heard it said that when you meet a true entrepreneur you can tell by talking to them that they are up to something. Just like a train that takes a lot of effort to get going, once it is in motion it is a force to be reckoned with. Just imagine when that is you; just imagine when you become Unstoppable!

You have created your 1-3-5 Action Plan. You created your Vision first, then your 3 Core Objectives and finally your 5 Goals for each Core Objective. The magic really starts to happen when you begin to use it.

Turn everything on its head

When you start using your 1-3-5 Action Plan we need to turn the whole thing on its head. By this I mean that you're going to work on a daily basis on the 5 Goals for each Core Objective, then they will lead to completing your 3 Core Objectives and they will enable you to achieve your Vision. So, although you created your 1-3-5, in execution it becomes 5-3-1.

I recommend that you download your 1-3-5 template using the link above and then fill it out. Mine sits in my top drawer and I look at it every single week on a Monday morning before I begin work for the week. If you want you could put a version on your laptop or tablet so it's always near.

I want you to do the same. I want you to have it close at hand so that you are regularly reading your Vision. Because you have followed the process your Vision is not just going to be corporate and just about your business. Your Vision has a personal element and that will remind you of your WHY. This stage cannot be emphasized enough. It's critical that you remember WHY. If you lose sight of your WHY your focus will slip and shortly thereafter so will your effectiveness.

One of your new successful habits is to create time so that at least once a week, preferably at the beginning, you read your full 1-3-5 Action Pan. Reading your Vision will excite you. Reading your Core Objectives will remind you what to focus on that month and week. Reading your goals and, if you're really serious about making this work, regularly writing out your main goal(s) you're going to work on on a pad or small piece of card will multiply your progress massively. Please don't complete the exercises above and your 1-3-5 and then leave it in a drawer or file. You'll only be able to become Unstoppable if you take action. During my Triathlon training, I was following a plan. Each day there were certain training sessions to complete for each discipline, which for me were my 3 Core Objectives. One of the benefits of maintaining a training diary is that you are always looking at what you are doing, what you plan to do and the progress you have made by doing. Remember Darren Hardy's success formula? It's about consistency.

Don't read your 1-3-5 and then leave it for weeks even months on end. Keep it close to hand and review it regularly. When would be a good time to plan some time in your diary so you review your 1-3-5 at least weekly?

Being self-disciplined means doing what you need to do, when you need to do it, whether you want to or not.

I want to briefly mention discipline here. We have to get serious about discipline. Being focused means that you are disciplined about what needs to be done. On occasion you'll find yourself facing an 'Action Pause'. It's these moments that will determine what your future is going to be. Being able to focus on what needs doing now, even though you may not want to do it, above what you would like to do because it is easier is what makes winners. No one has achieved success without being disciplined. Being self-disciplined means doing what you need to do, when you need to do it, whether you want to or not. If you are to achieve your grand Vision that you have written in your 1-3-5 Action Plan, you have to be disciplined. Stick to the cause, stick to the plan and be focused on your 1-3-5. I find that by removing emotion from certain decisions about what to do helps with my discipline. Sometimes we decide that we don't feel like doing that task. We know that it needs to be done. This is where emotion comes into it. Just because you don't want to do something isn't a good enough reason not to do it; you're becoming Unstoppable. Take emotion out of the equation and just get on with the task. If you can do this consistently on the things that really matter you will be disciplined and make progress. Coming up in Part Three are the key skills that you're going to develop in order to make the absolute best of yourself and your 1-3-5 Action Plan.

Just because you don't want to do something isn't a good enough reason not to do it.

Here's what Mike Weedon from Life Cover For All said about his 1-3-5 Action Plan:

I, like most business owners, spent a huge amount of (wasted) time writing a detailed business plan but had never got round to updating it as it was such a time consuming job and things have changed so much since I formed the company. Then I found the 1-3-5. Having a focused 1-3-5 gives me a usable, real-time snapshot of the past, present and more importantly the future! It's easy to change the focus or goal slightly – knowing that they are all contributing to my Vision and Objectives.

❗ Key Development Point

Get serious about discipline and be focused on your 1-3-5. Get some time planned in your diary to have a regular spot for your 1-3-5 Action Plan.

Part Three

The Execution Skills

6

The Four Key Skills You Need

There are many skills that are needed in order to become a success. There are, however, some key ones that I'm going to focus on here. I have found from experience and from the results my clients have delivered that these four key skills will bring the best outcome for you and your business. The four key skills are the skills that I needed to work on when I was training for my Ultra Endurance Triathlon and these are the key skills when I want to focus on developing my business.

I needed to improve my leadership because I had to build a clear picture of what I was going to achieve. I have to engage myself regularly, especially before a 3-hour run! By focusing on my clear picture I trained consistently. I had to get better at delivery and execution because I couldn't just think myself fit, I had to physically get out there and do the training. I recently responded to a tweet from Tom Peters (@tom_peters) about leadership and accountability. He replied that 'leading yourself may be toughest of all'. I believe this to be true. It's all too easy to let yourself off, to ease back and never ever flick the cruise control switch! Tom said to me that he was brutal on himself. Jim Rohn (an entrepreneur, author and motivational speaker, www.jimrohn.com) said in *The Art of Exceptional Living* 'that if you work hard on your job you'll make a living but if you work hard on yourself you'll make a fortune'.

⟨?⟩ Key Question

The key question many of us need to ask ourselves more often is 'if I was the very best version of myself, what could I achieve?' When you answer this you must do something about it!

Next, I had to work on my Personal Organization. One of the major obstacles that you face when you are training for Ultra Endurance events or building a business/career is time. With Endurance events you have to be training between 8 and 18 hours a week. At the time I did my Triathlon I was married with two daughters and had a demanding business. Eighteen hours a week is like having a part-time job. I had to get very good at finding time to train and make sure that the training I did was effective.

This is the same as in your business – be clear about what you want to achieve from each task. Outcome thinking comes into play here. Before I started anything I had to be clear about the outcome I wanted. I didn't really have to consider my client relationships when I was training but I did have to consider my family relationships.

Training long and hard does have an impact on your family life and when it is time with the family I had to make sure that was 'quality time'. It was no good spending time with my wife and reading *220 Triathlon* (a triathlon magazine) at the same time. Also, if I was watching a film with my two daughters I couldn't do core strength work at the same time. Anyone who is in a relationship realizes that the negotiation of time and effort with their significant other is a critical step in deciding to really go for an Endurance Triathlon. Isn't it the same in launching and running a business? Yeah, the rewards can be great but you do need to put the effort in.

Finally, I had strength development. I don't mean physical strength development here (although that was fairly important), I mean the areas that I was naturally strong in. I had suffered a groin strain earlier from running and was naturally fairly strong on the bike. Because of these two factors my training time was built around the bike and at times felt like I lived on the thing! I worked hard in order to get off the bike in a reasonably fresh state. Of course, I couldn't neglect the other two disciplines but it made sense to focus on my bike strength. This also is the same in your business; make sure your strengths are identified and fully utilized.

So the four key execution skills that make up the remaining elements of your Unstoppable system are:

1. Leadership

2. Personal Organization

3. Relationship Building

4. Key Strength Development

1. Leadership

For me you cannot make the best of yourself and your circumstances without developing your leadership skills. Even if you are a micro-sized professional, how you lead yourself is critical. If you are unable to work alone or if you do have a team to support you, how you lead your-self and others will determine your level of success. Habit 7 in Stephen Covey's book *The 7 Habits of Highly Effective People* is 'Sharpen the saw'. This certainly applies to your leadership skills; these need to be continually sharpened.

After you have developed your leadership skills it is very important that you make the most of your time. I cannot tell you how many times business owners and professionals have told me that 'they don't have the time'. It's an excuse that I have used in the past as well.

! Key Development Point

I learnt this and it made a big difference. If we needed more time, the day would obviously be longer. Clearly, it is long enough!

2. Personal Organization

Personal Organization is a skill that I have invested many hours in developing. I'm still not perfect, I'm not sure anyone is, but I'm in a place that I'm getting far more done. I'm concentrating on the important stuff and avoid wasting my precious time. Plus, through establishing time blocks I get in the zone more often.

3. Relationship Building

Focusing in relationships is key. I read an article in *Management Today* magazine a short while ago that confirmed my belief: they said that 'companies that understand the importance of customer relationship management are going to be the first companies out of the recession'. All too often I see business owners putting great emphasis on the transaction. I understand the importance of a slick sales process as much as anyone but the emphasis should be on the relationship and not the transaction. Skill number three is getting better at strengthening and deepening of your relationships.

4. Key Strength Development

Once you have become a better leader and are engaging those who can support you to deliver more, once you have learned how to make the very best of your 86,500 seconds each day and you have found creative ways to develop and strengthen your relationships, it's time to work on your key strengths. We all have key strengths and the degree to which we utilize and set our businesses up to make use of this key strength will be the final piece in achieving your grand Vision and making the very most of yourself.

It is important to stress here that we are not looking to become perfect in any of these skills; we are looking only to make progress in these areas in order to make the very best of our 1-3-5 Action Plan. That is the only reason we are going to work on these skills.

7

Skill One: Leadership

What is leadership? Leadership for me is keeping things as simple as they can be. It's not about overcomplicating things – it's about results. It's about achieving the big picture. It's about deciding what result your organization, your family or your sports club want to achieve and it's about engaging yourself and those around you with effective communication to 'come on board' and deliver that result.

Steve Radcliffe in his simple book called *Future Engage Deliver* talks about that very process, Future, Engage and Deliver. He said that with all his experience of working within large organizations as a chief executive and then as a leadership coach, he realized that we make leadership more complex than it is.

I agree with Steve and also that, as an effective leader, you need to be thinking about the future.

Key Question

In the last week, how much structured time have you spent thinking about your future or your business future?

You see, the first thing I want to emphasize is that in order for you to reach your Vision of success you need to be thinking about it. If you are like most of the business owners that I come across you probably answered that question with not much effort. Earlier I said that the reason your business is doing so well is because of you but also the reason your business is only doing so well is also because of you. If you're going to achieve great things, wouldn't it be a great idea to spend time thinking and working on those things?

I don't want to give you an actual figure of how many hours you should be spending thinking about your Vision and your business future because that is up to you, but I would say that a lot of your thinking should be in the future. When I ran my retail business it was up to me to think where we needed to be, what suppliers we would need to bring on board, what the team should look like and what skills gaps we had. It was a small business and I needed to be close to the business, working in it a great deal but still consciously pulling myself out of it on a regular basis to work on it.

When I was a company sales manager with a team of 30 store managers I needed to ensure that the future (largely made up of a juicy sales target) was clear and that I spent time thinking about how we were going to reach and exceed it.

I know what it is like to fire fight and react to demands from customers but I want to stress that if you aren't thinking and making decisions about your Vision no one else is. Sure we can develop other people's leadership skills and if you're leading a team you'll want them to deliver the results, but spend time thinking about your future, it's your Vision after all.

I'm sure we've all been around exceptional leaders. You know that feeling when someone spends a little time with you or perhaps you've just been around them in a meeting but you instantly feel better? You feel more confident and your belief increases and you find yourself wanting to reach bigger and bigger goals. What you've experienced is a leader who is fully connected to their Vision of success. They have a clear idea of what they want to create, what success looks like and what they want to create really matters to them. Their enthusiasm and confidence that they or the business is going to get there is contagious, isn't it? That's what we are looking to create here. So, when you have completed your Vision and you've made it personal to the things that matter to you, now is the stage to communicate to those around you what the Vision is. Now I'm not suggesting you upset people by telling them how you want them to work like mad so that you can swim in your pool in Mexico, but you can enthuse them with the idea of success and how this will positively impact them.

A simple way in which I was successful as a leader was to motivate my team to deliver the business Vision by linking it to what they cared about. I found out by taking a genuine interest in what mattered to them. For some it may have been a money bonus to buy a new car. For others it was time off to spend with their families. Some of my managers were motivated by advancement and the chance to learn new skills and then play a bigger part in the business. The key thing was that I realized that these managers were vital to my achieving success, and by making them feel involved, because we were a team, meant the future was more secure.

I suggested earlier that the reason why it was important for you to read your 1-3-5 Action Plan each week ideally at the start is for you to reconnect with your Vision. When you spend even a short while reading your

Vision, imaging what it's like because you've achieved and what you'll feel like, you'll find the experience massively rewarding. What you are doing is simply spending time in the future.

Who do I engage?

If you're leading a team you obviously need to engage them. This is easier said than done. I recall a session a while ago when I started working with a professional team. During the first session I pulled everyone together. In the briefing room were two directors and seven support people. I wanted to inform everyone at the beginning of the coaching programme what the process was going to be, what the outcomes were going to be and how everyone working together would enable better results. That first session was very difficult to say the least. I was trying to communicate the future, which at the time was just the desired outcome of the coaching programme, and I wanted to engage everyone. It was clear that the reason the session was so difficult was because up to that point there hadn't been much engagement with the team at all. There was a feeling of them and us. That was one of the main reasons why the business wasn't performing at the required level.

In this case the directors were not aware of what to do. In some cases I've seen business owners be very technically competent in the product the business delivers but leadership is a skill in itself. In the area of leadership they fall short. That is why leadership is a key skill in developing your becoming Unstoppable.

Once we had completed more sessions with the whole team they opened up and began to bring ideas to the session that enabled the business to move towards the Vision at a faster pace. The little difference made a big difference and the team was now engaged.

So, the first people you engage if you have a team are the team. Ask yourself now how well have you engaged your team? Be honest. Does your team know where you are heading? Does your team know what progress has been made and how they are performing? Do you have a structured performance management process in place where good performance is reward and poor performance is highlighted and acted upon? When was the last time you held a team meeting? Was there an agenda? Did you do all the talking or did you ask what needs people have and look to supporting them to meet those needs? How well do you know your team? If I was to turn up Monday morning and ask how engaged were your team in what you are doing, what would they say?

These may seem like obvious questions but I can assure you that these questions are not being asked in many businesses. When you develop your leadership skills and actually 'lead' your team, you'll be light years ahead, plus you'll find it easier because with an engaged team you'll start to develop leaders at all levels of the business structure.

I'm very passionate about giving people feedback when I'm leading them. In the past I've practised a fairly robust process of ensuring people know how they are performing, how they are contributing and giving them the opportunity to request support to perform better or develop a new skill. This is the system that I've used. If you want to make it simpler and have fewer levels, that's up to you. What is key is that you have 'something' in place rather than nothing.

So, if you are going to communicate effectively with your team to ensure they are engaged, this system works. Remember, communication or rather lack of it continues to be a major challenge within businesses. For now I want you to think about internal communications. I've used this four-stage system for a long time now. First, it's a system that has been tested. Second, people know where they are and have the opportunity to engage with the business Vision. Lastly, it's a two-way process, so you'll start to receive golden nuggets from your team.

Here's the four-stage system:

1. A very short, 2–4-minute informal chat called a KIT (keep in touch) conducted weekly.

2. A slightly longer, 15–20-minute monthly 121. This is where you begin a structure of what you want to cover. It could be sales performance, quality control or general results. Here you are looking to engage the person in the business Vision and let them know what they are doing well, and if relevant some areas to improve.

3. A quarterly review with more detail lasting 30–45 minutes. Here we are even more formal and the team member is encouraged to prepare for this session. An action plan may be discussed here. This stage really is about performance on the job.

4. An annual appraisal lasting about an hour. Completely structured, these are a great way to reward a great performance year and set some stretch goals for the person to achieve next year. The annual appraisal is planned and follows set guidelines. I have a client and their website, www.fingertipsolutions.org.uk, has some great resources that can help with your appraisals.

So there you have it, a simple four-stage system to ensure that your people know what is happening, how they are contributing and what needs to be achieved for the future.

It all falls down with execution

The final stage of Steve Radcliffe's essential guide to your leadership is Deliver. I'm sure you've experienced as a customer a business that doesn't deliver. I love pizza and no matter how shiny the menu is, how much time the chef takes in making my pizza, even supposing he remembers to put extra pepperoni and jalapeños on, it all falls down if the delivery driver gets lost and my pizza isn't delivered. How about on a larger scale? How about you've decided to buy a new car, maybe lease one for your business? You get the car, you enjoy driving it and it's reliable. Then comes the time to get your car serviced. You turn up at the garage, drop it off and are told that it'll be ready by 5pm. You go back to collect the car and they tell you it's not ready. From a service point of view they failed to deliver. Now, if you have a meeting the next day 200 miles away, how clean the car is or how you like it doesn't matter because the garage didn't deliver.

My wife recently ordered a new mobility scooter for her father. On the due date of delivery it didn't come, so we called the delivery number but didn't get a great deal of joy. Upon checking their website I read something that actually made me laugh. One of their core statements was, and I quote, 'We promise to keep our promises'. What is that about? The scooter wasn't delivered and they were a delivery company that hadn't called us to let us know why. Clearly, these guys fell down with execution. Look at your own business for a moment. Are there any areas where the product is great, the service during the sales process is great but your delivery lets your customer down? Is there an area where you could enhance the delivery of your product or service? It's your job as the leader to check and see that these critical things are improved.

When you and your business don't deliver, that's the effect; it can all fall short of your potential. You really let yourself, your business and most of your clients down. So, if you're going to become a better leader, you and your team, if you have one, have to follow through and deliver.

Being able to execute is essential. There are times when you are doing things in your business that are not glamorous. There will be times when you as the leader may want to do something else, and being the leader may mean that no one is going to kick you in the backside if you don't execute.

This is why you need to build and develop this part of your leadership. If you don't follow through and execute, it's not fair to your team or your customers.

Being able to execute is essential. The ability to execute is certainly helped by having your 1-3-5 Action Plan. With practice you will become very connected to your Vision and will be building your WHY power. But that's not enough. You need a measurement process in place so that you can hold yourself accountable for the things that need to be done. This could be a simple spreadsheet of your key performance indicators (KPIs). If you are following through and executing on a consistent basis, then what results will you see? Could there be a sales target, a certain result from your marketing plan or an improvement in your overall margin levels? This is personal to you, but have something in place so you can lead yourself.

If your team has got a problem with execution you need to find the cause. The first place to look is being critical about the job you did when you communicated your Vision. Have you shared where the business is heading? Did you engage the team or were they left alone and resistant, like the team I described in my example? It may be that there is a motivation or training issue. If you are measuring and monitoring your performance as Peter Drucker said, then you will see evidence that your business is not executing.

A system I put in place with a client a while ago was a simple feedback postcard. We were keen to get an understanding of the level of service we were delivering. After a new client had been on board with them for a month we sent them a postcard. On the postcard was a simple request: 'Please rate the service you have received for the last month from 1–10, with 1 being poor and 10 being excellent. If you can't give us a 10 please let us know what we can do to get a 10.'

You wouldn't believe the feedback we received. We didn't always receive a 10 but we had excellent feedback on how to improve our delivery in order to get a 10. It also was an excellent way to demonstrate to our customers that we took delivery seriously.

Mini leadership review

Here are some questions I'd like you to think about and answer. In running your business or department you've probably learned a great deal. You probably have some great leadership skills already but you may not be applying these skills and habits consistently.

1. Thinking about the future of your business or life, how clear are you about its future? Do you know specifically where you are heading? Is your Vision crystal clear? (Are you engaged with your Vision, are you 'living it'?)

2. How much time have you spent in the last month engaging your direct team, if you have one, in your Vision? (Do your people know where they are going and how they are currently performing?)

3. Who are the members of your support team? Who can you go to for advice and support about your business? Do you have a support team with a good mix of skills and abilities? (You don't have to go it alone; synergize with different people, even those outside your business.)

4. When was the last time you critically assessed your business's ability to deliver your product or service? (Look at your business through the eyes of your clients.)

5. What developments have you implemented in the last 30 days to the delivery of your product or service? (We should be constantly looking to improve our delivery.)

It's important that we regularly pause and check the direction we are heading in and assess our performance at the top of our business.

I heard a beautiful example of where we should check with ourselves recently from Darren Hardy, he said: 'When a plane takes off it is more often than not off plan. It constantly assesses, using a gyroscope, its projected direction and corrects itself to stay on track. If it didn't, by the end of its journey it could be 150 miles off course.' We should do the same.

I'm a member of the Entrepreneurs Forum, which has its base in Newcastle upon Tyne in the North East of England. One of the benefits of belonging to the forum, in addition to being able to build a fantastic support team, is that you get to see and hear great leaders presenting. I remember a session led by Jeff Grout, the leadership coach. In his session, Jeff suggested learning from our past and shared four excellent questions. These four questions have certainly helped me, and here they are:

1. What are the good things you do that you must keep doing?

2. What are the good things you know you must start doing?

3. What are the things you do occasionally that you must do consistently?

4. What are the bad things you do that you must stop doing?

I learned a great deal when I answered these questions properly. I've seen people only scrape the surface with these. I suggest you set aside some time and really look into the answers you come up with.

You see, there will be good things that you did recently, maybe last year. When you are analysing your business and your performance you really need to identify these things. The risk is that you did something in the past and this produced a good result. You need to build a system so that you keep doing these things.

Another benefit of answering this question thoroughly is that you reconnect with the good things you do. Later on you can refer to these things when we talk about communicating your value.

Complacency has damaged many businesses. When a business stops doing the good things it used to do it loses sales, profit, customers and market share. Could that be the reason why IBM is no longer a major player in the home PC market? Could that be the reason why Sony televisions were caught up and then overtaken by a smaller company called Samsung? Could that be the reason why Nokia, who were a major player in the mobile phone market, lost out to BlackBerry and iPhone?

From a sporting point of view, what happens to Rocky in *Rocky 3* when he stops doing what he used to do in his training? He gets beaten by Clubber Lang. He then revisits the basics and wins back the title. I know strictly speaking that Rocky isn't real (I think more of us should follow his lead though) but you'll get the point.

Spend a little time working out the good things you do that you must keep doing.

So spend a little time working out the good things you do that you must keep doing.

As for the second question, what are the good things that you must start doing? Don't just make a list of things; think about it a little more. If one of the good things you should start doing is social media, what specifically could you do? Could you work with a social media trainer and get some support? When I answered this question, I decided to work with a social media coach, Karen James (KLJ Social Media), and Karen developed a strategy and implementation programme for me. I approached it strategically with specific outcomes and tracked my progress.

Another one for me was to demonstrate value up front without risk to my suspects or prospects. I designed a free action book and set up a landing page on my website. This enabled me to offer excellent value along with capturing people's names and email addresses to begin a relationship.

What are the things you need to start doing? Do you follow up well? Should you build your support team? Should you network strategically?

Question 3 brought loads of things to light for me. One of the biggest was direct mail. I had in the past sent out direct mail letters to people and companies that I identified could benefit from my coaching and development. When I checked, one such letter had generated £1000s of sales. But for some reason I'd stopped sending out the letters. Maybe I broke the habit, maybe I didn't measure sufficiently or maybe I got lazy. The fact is that it had worked for me, but I hadn't done it consistently and that needed to be changed.

I then looked at my networking success. I realized that when I fully prepared for a networking meeting with a great '60-second introduction' I got better results. To be honest, on occasions in the past I had winged it. I'd been busy and just didn't prepare properly. That also changed and I now always have something prepared and an outcome in mind.

So look back, what has worked in the past? What brought a return but for some reason you stopped doing it? Being consistent is key; the tortoise always wins the race. If you look at the different areas of your life, your relationships, your health and your business, could you say that if you had been consistent your results would be better?

I'm certain you'll come up with a load of things, appraisals, weekly team meetings, developing connector relationships, rewarding yourself for your successes or having holidays!

When you have completed your 1-3-5 Action Plan you'll have identified your 5 Goals for each Core Objective. These are the areas that you need to move from doing occasionally to doing consistently.

When I answered question 4, at first I thought I didn't do any bad things. Then I looked a little deeper. A bad thing I did a while ago was to sell myself short. I read a great book called *The Magic of Thinking Big* by David Schwartz. In his book he has a chapter titled 'You are better than you think you are'; the following chapter is titled 'You are twice as good as you think you are'. WOW! Those two chapters made a big difference to me. If I was twice as good as I thought I was, what could I achieve?

Have you ever sold yourself short? Have you ever charged less for your service because you sold yourself short? If you have, what are you going to do about it? What simple action to move you a little further on can you take today?

Another bad thing I did that I had to stop doing was being late. I used to underestimate how long something would take me to complete, then I would overestimate how fast I could drive from one place to the next and then underestimate how many red lights I'd get while driving! The result was simple: I was late, I was stressed and I'd come over as unprofessional. I'd let myself and others down.

Have a good think about what the bad things are you do that you must stop doing. What impact are these things having on you? Are they affecting your confidence, your business or your results?

Some clients have told me they are going to stop overpromising and then putting themselves under pressure. Others have said that a bad thing they do is to allow unrealistic expectations from their clients. They felt they had to respond within minutes. As a result they piled the pressure on themselves and then couldn't do what they had planned to do.

You don't answer this question to kick yourself, you answer this question so that you can learn and develop.

The purpose of answering these questions is to learn about how you have led yourself. It's not enough just to be good at your job or role.

It's vital that you become the best leader you can be and that involves learning from how you've operated in the past.

Leadership communication

How well do you communicate? Being a good communicator is an essential component of effective leadership. A short while ago I completed my Certificate in the Art and Science of Neuro Linguistic Programming (NLP). I did this in the North East with a lady called Cricket Kemp (North East NLP) and the course really helped my communication and how I led myself. NLP has been described by some as having a manual for your brain. It is a model that was developed in the 1970s by Richard Bandler and John Grinder. These men identified that certain therapists using the same tools as others achieved far better results. Bandler and Grinder realized that there were some common characteristics between these master communicators. From these they developed NLP.

There are many good books on NLP and a detailed description is beyond the remit of this book. My intention is to give you an insight into how I use NLP to perform as a leader better, and whet your appetite so that you may look at it in more detail.

NLP has four pillars. These four pillars are the foundation of NLP, they are:

- Rapport

- Sensory Awareness

- Behavioural Flexibility

- Outcome Thinking

Why is it that you just get on with some people more than others? Why is it that you seem to connect with some people more than others?

The answer lies in Rapport. From a leadership communication point of view, if you can learn to develop rapport with your team or your clients, then you'll achieve better results. It's important to emphasize that these skills are to be used ethically. If you listen to the types of words people use you'll notice that some use 'visual' words such as 'I see what you mean' or 'the future looks bright'. When communicating with this type of person you should use similar phrases. Another person may say 'that rings a bell' or 'yeah, I understand, loud and clear'. These people may be predominantly 'auditory'. They use sound words; again you would match their usage. Finally, there are people who are 'kinaesthetic'. They use words that are all about feeling. 'I have a good feeling about this project' or 'something tells me we shouldn't go ahead'. If you were talking to a predominantly kinaesthetic person and you keep saying 'you're not seeing the point', they're thinking 'no I'm not because I need to feel the point'. It would be much better to say 'how does that feel?' In simple terms, listen to what people are saying, the words they are using and match those words.

You can also match body language. If someone is sitting with folded arms, you can match them; if they have their legs crossed, you can match that also. If you want to check this works, an extreme example is to sit opposite someone and match their body language and then lean right back in your chair and stretch your legs out. If you watch them while you are doing this you'll notice how uncomfortable they are. The reason for this is because you've just broken rapport with them.

There are other ways you can build rapport, such as the tone and pace of your voice. The point is that if you can get 'into rapport' with people, then they are more likely to be influenced by you.

Sensory awareness is great. At the obvious end of the scale, I know as soon as I come home from the office if I have forgotten to do something for my wife. Sharon doesn't have to say anything but I know from the way she is that something is not right. I'm sure you've felt that before.

Well, when we're communicating as leaders the people we are com-municating to will be sending us the same type of signals. Building your sensory awareness skills will enable you to read these signals and act on them. You'll begin to notice if one member of your team hasn't done something because their neck goes slightly red when you ask them about it. It may be that another finds it difficult to maintain eye contact when you ask them if they have hit their sales target. You can begin to 'calibrate' people and when you notice what you are saying is making them act in a certain way you may have to change your approach.

This brings us to Behavioural Flexibility. Many of us are creatures of habit. We operate in our own rigid way. When we communicate or manage people we always do it the same way regardless of whether one person likes to be communicated to in a different way. Do you always put the same shoe on in the morning? Do you always brush your teeth with the same hand? Do you always drive to work the same way and then sit in the same seat in the boardroom? If you do, then it would be worth you building the habit of becoming more flexible. When you see break-downs in a company such as a pay deal it is normally because of a lack of flexibility. You can decide to be more flexible. If what you are doing is not working, then do something different. It sounds simple but many people end up doing the same thing in their business they did last week and expect a different result. It isn't going to work!

If you're talking to one of your team or one of your clients and the conversation isn't going the way you expected, if you have Behavioural Flexibility then you can adapt your communication and come from or see things from a different angle. Wouldn't that be a good thing?

Finally, we have Outcome Thinking. This one pillar alone has made a really big difference to the way I operate. Outcome Thinking is about always having an outcome in mind. You know when you've had that 40-minute phone conversation and after you have finished and put the phone down you say to yourself 'what was the point of that' or 'I didn't get clarity on where we are with…'; Outcome Thinking eliminates that. It means you're a better leader and communicator because you know what success looks like from any situation. Referring again to Stephen Covey's excellent book *The 7 Habits of Highly Effective People*, habit 2 is 'begin with the end in mind'. This is very similar to Outcome Thinking. The principle is that before you start something, a meeting, a project or a conversation, you must have an outcome in mind.

Putting them all together

When you put all four pillars together, you realize how magnificent they are. When you become skilled at building rapport, people feel comfortable around you and they feel you're on their wavelength. When you add sensory awareness to that, then you're more in tune with the effect your communication is having on them. If that isn't the desired effect, you have behavioural flexibility skills to change or adapt your approach and begin to see things from a different or even maybe their angle. Plus, because before the conversation even started you had a clear outcome in mind, the likelihood of reaching that outcome is greatly increased. All of this leads to you becoming a more effective leader and with your being a more effective leader you'll improve your business results.

If NLP has resonated with you, I've written a short blog on 'The 13 Operating Beliefs of NLP'; you can read it at www.petewilkinson.com/blog.

Finally, your own personal brand as a leader is largely influenced by your reputation. This is an area often overlooked by many people. Your reputation is developed by three main areas, these are:

1. What you say

2. What you do

3. What others say about you

It is worth spending a little time looking at these and deciding what you can do to positively influence them. For example, how often have you said something damaging that affected your reputation? Gerald Ratner (the former Chief Executive of the major British jewellery company Ratners Group) literally lost millions by something he said about the products his business supplied.

I'm sure you've also seen the actions of someone damage their business. A well-known coffee shop in early 2013 paid a high price for something they did in relation to tax and in return their image for a time was reportedly damaged.

The third area is more interesting. Here it is a case of consciously making a decision to positively influence what others say about you. Obvious ways are how companies utilize PR. But there are other ways that are possibly less expensive for small business owners. How can you become a perceived expert in your area? What could you produce and then share to demonstrate your expertise? Both of these strategies are effective in impacting what others say about you that will in turn develop your reputation. It's also worth noting that this is one of the most powerful ways to build a reputation. From my own experience, I wrote a short pocket action book that people can download for free. It's a great way to build my reputation by influencing what people say about me.

Leadership is the first skill that needs to be developed in becoming Unstoppable; it will enable you to develop the ability to make the very most of your 1-3-5 Action Plan.

Your progress so far!

So, at this point you will have created your 1-3-5 Action Plan. You'll have a clear picture of what success looks like to you. You will have identified your 3 Core Objectives so that you have a monthly focus and your Core

Objectives will keep you on track. You have identified 5 Goals that are action orientated that frame your every week and day. You work on the tasks so that you achieve your goals that feed into your Core Objectives. Once you have achieved your 3 Core Objectives you will achieve your Vision. You'll be smiling and happy because with your Vision you have the life and business that you want. You now have worked on becoming a better leader. You now realize that even if the only person you lead is yourself, how well you lead yourself will determine what the things are you focus on. As you become a better leader you will start to build your support team so that you can accelerate your progress. You understand that you want momentum on your side and people will start to notice that you are up to something. That something is your Vision. You also appreciate that your Vision is so big and grand that it scares normal people. That's part of the process because you are in control of what you do and you have taken full responsibility for creating the life and business that you want.

 Key Development Point

Understand that the toughest challenge of all is how you lead yourself; be brutal on yourself.

8

Skill Two: Personal Organization

This for me was an absolute game changer. It was an area that I wasn't great at and worked really hard to get to where I am now. For me it's far more than just time management, which in itself is funny as we can't actually manage time – just what we do with our time.

As I mentioned earlier, whenever I do a keynote presentation I always ask the audience if anyone has had one of those days where they are really busy putting in loads of effort but at the end of the day they've achieved absolutely nothing. On every occasion nearly everyone raises their hand. So it's clear that for most people this is a challenge and an area that needs developing. To start with, complete these simple self-assessment questionnaires and see where you are at:

The Self Assessment Questionnaire

I tend to tackle paperwork the first time I see it

Yes   No

Do you have a do-it-now mindset?

I face more crises than I need to because of poor planning

Yes   No

I'm often in the urgent/important quadrant and feel pressure

I sometimes have to be chased by others to get things done

Yes   No

Do I have to be pushed by others to stay on task?

I have a vague idea of what my priorities are

Yes   No

Have you worked out your key business and life priorities?

I spend more than 30 minutes a day looking for things

Yes   No

My office/work environment is disorganized

(Continued)

My meetings tend to last longer than necessary

Yes   No

I am not outcome focused and lose track of time!

I allow others to negatively influence how I spend my time

Yes   No

I am not always in control of what happens to me!

I start a lot more projects than I finish

Yes   No

I am easily distracted chasing bright blue butterflies

I am always busy but not always productive

Yes   No

I never stop, I'm so busy but achieve very little

I hang on to tasks that should be delegated

Yes   No

I have to do everything myself because no one's better

The purpose of completing this self-analysis is to begin the process of assessing where you are now with your relationship with time. It's a way of seeing if you waste time or invest time.

Every single day you get 86,400 seconds to use how you wish.

Every single day you get 86,400 seconds to use how you wish. How effective are you at utilizing your time?

Get control of yourself at the start of your week

The very beginning of being personally organized is to fully utilize your 1-3-5 Action Plan. Ideally, you would read your 1-3-5 on a Monday morning to frame your week. You're reading it to reconnect with your Vision and understand why you're doing whatever it is you're doing. You are reminding yourself what the big picture is and what has to be done on a monthly, weekly and daily basis to achieve the big picture; doing this one vital step alone will put you in an effective state to make the most of your time. Imagine when you really believe you're destined for great things and you have this exciting Vision that is just there in front of you. You can see it, you know what it is going to feel like when you achieve it and you know how your clients, you and your family are going to benefit from it. This is your motivational juice to keep you on track. When you start with this at the beginning of the week you just know that you want to make the very best of your 86,400 seconds!

Why is it that some people just seem to get more done? Is it because they are luckier? Is it because they have a larger team? The reason some people just seem to get more done is because:

- They plan.

- They stay focused.

- They work on what's important not urgent.

- They are consistent.

● They manage their distractions.

● They are clear about what they want to achieve.

Let's look inside for a moment. How well do you plan? Do you plan at all? When I work with clients in this area it's amazing how many don't have an effective diary system set up. Your diary system doesn't need to be electronic (although the one I use now is). It doesn't have to be complex with bells and whistles. It just has to work for you!

So how do you plan? The first thing to understand is that you should plan for at least one week at a time. It is not effective to come into the business in the morning and think 'what should I do today'. That is not making the most of your time. Because you have developed the successful habit of reading your 1-3-5 Action Plan at least every week you'll know what you should be working on.

The first thing is to formulate a plan of what you are going to do. It's best to do this at the end of the previous week. Maybe do it last task on a Friday afternoon or on a Sunday night. At the absolute latest do it on a Monday morning if you're an early bird.

OK, it's Friday afternoon and you're planning next week, what do you do? Well, first get out your 1-3-5 and look at your 3 Core Objectives. Which one is going to be the major focus for the upcoming week? The purpose of your 3 Core Objectives is to keep you on track on a monthly basis. So you know which Core Objective it's going to be. Then you look at your 5 action orientated Goals and pick the one or few that you are going to progress with. There will be some tasks that need to be completed so that you can achieve these goals. This is the stuff that you will be working on when you have dedicated 'working on your business time blocks'. I'll mention these again later but briefly I've used time blocks a lot and they are simple to set up. I simply look at my diary and block out sections of time that are anything from 30 minutes to a few hours. These time blocks are protected and I get really clear what I want to achieve out of them. Having time blocks set up means that you remove all distractions and get yourself in a flow. That means no Facebook or Twitter, no email or phone calls. Disconnect and be prepared to be surprised how much you can achieve.

After you have identified the goals that you are working on and the tasks that need to be completed to achieve your goals, you plan in your diary when you will do these activities. I use ACT (the Customer Relationship Management (CRM) software programme from Sage) for my diary. I would then log into ACT and for each day decide which are my three VITs (very important things). I write my three VIT's in red so that they stand out; that's up to you. My three VITs are the things that I know will enable me to make progress. They have been driven from the Goals that were driven from the Core Objectives that were driven from the Vision. This means that everything is aligned.

So, in practical terms you'll end up with a full week where each day you have allocated some time to work 'on' your business, which is time to work 'on' your 1-3-5. Just sit for a few minutes and imagine it's Friday afternoon and next week is fully laid out with 15 tasks (your VITs over 5 days), and you know that when you complete these 15 tasks you'll have made progress. Doesn't that feel great? I'm not saying every minute of every day has to be planned but we do need to get control of our time.

This is the first step in being personally organized, making sure that you plan and give yourself a chance to achieve success. In the real world I know all sorts of things go on. I know that there are crises and emergencies and urgent stuff that just happen. But if we are to get control of how we operate and make the most of our time and resources, then we need to set ourselves up. Doing the activity of planning to work on the important things at the end of the week or at the latest early Monday morning is an area we need to be disciplined in.

I'm sure you've had days that just fly by and before you know it it's 5pm. When you form the habit of having at least your week planned you'll be way ahead. The next thing after you've planned your week is to develop a start-of-day and end-of-day routine.

When I was working in retail there were certain jobs that had to be done first thing in a morning. Maybe that was changing the security tapes, putting the floats in the tills, tidying the tickets or updating the sales board, you get the picture. There were also things that had to be done at the end of the day. You had to shut down the computer system, ring through your sales figures to head office, spend 15 minutes on centre leadership (this is where you look after a certain area of the store and ensure the standards are high before you leave for the day). Now, in between all of that the day could be crazy and often was but you started and ended the day well.

Look at your own life, what success routine have you developed to start and end the day, or to start and end the week, month or quarter?

So, after you have planned at least your week with your three VITs for each day, develop a simple routine to start and finish your day. If this is a new concept for you, set yourself up to win. Start with a really easy and straightforward routine that you know you can maintain. You can build it once you have the habit of completing the simple routine first. Brian Tracy recommends that you start the day by writing out your three major goals. Brendon Burchard (author, public speaker and online trainer, www.brendonburchard.com) recommends that you decide what you want to achieve, who you need to talk to and make sure you have all of your resources to hand. Darren Hardy was woken up every morning at 6am by his father doing his start-of-day routine – weight training in the garage!

My start-of-day routine consists of a Monday reading my 1-3-5 Action Plan. I then decide what looks like a good week, what outcome I'd like for that week and where I'd like to be by Friday night. For the rest of the week my start-of-day routine consists of a look at ACT and ensuring I have my three VITs and have other tasks chunked together such as social media updates, or phone calls, or emails to write. I never ever check my email first thing in the morning until my day is planned and framed. At the end of each day I carry out a really quick review. Have all my tasks for the day been completed? Is there anything to carry forward? By doing this I am concentrating on what is important and giving myself the best opportunity of success.

Every day there are certain things that need to get done. There is an essay written by E.M. Gray called 'The Common Denominator of Success'. In it he observed that 'the successful person has the habit of doing the things failures don't like to do'.

One of the challenges I faced was that because I hadn't planned what I needed to do each day, whether that was send that letter, make that phone call, follow up with that prospect, write that article, or have that conversation, I filled my day with things that I thought I should be doing. Often these things were enjoyable but weren't the things that were going to enable me to make the most of what time I had and my potential. Now, everything is driven from my 1-3-5 Action Plan.

In the past you may have worked on the things you like to do rather than the things you know you should do. Some things in running our businesses just have to be done. They may not be enjoyable and they may cause us to push our comfort zones, but joined-up business running means we do these things.

Brian Tracy has a book called *Eat that Frog* where the basis is that each day we do the hard thing first and get it out of the way. We can then go on to enjoy the rest of the day. The fact is that many of us, including me in the past, focused on the nice stuff first, the stuff that made us feel good instantly, and at the end of the day we realized that we have run out of time and don't get that tough thing done. Sometimes that tough thing gets carried forward for many days.

When you develop your discipline to work on the things that need to be done, to do a few of the things each day that you might not want to do but you know need to be done, then you'll be surging ahead with your progress. Plus, you'll start to feel much better about yourself.

We've discussed how to plan your week using your 1-3-5 Action Plan as the driver. But did you know that if you turned the page of your diary or you scrolled over on ACT or Outlook that next week is already there? (I'm being a little cheeky here but you'd be surprised how many professional people I've met don't plan ahead.) If you really want to be personally organized and get a load more done, then you will build the habit of planning ahead more than just a week; you'll begin to plan a month and even 90 days ahead. Now, I'm not talking about having your three VITs done for the next 3 months. But I am talking about spending some time planning other actions and activities from your 1-3-5 Action Plan in your diary. As I mentioned briefly earlier, a simple strategy that has really worked for me is the use of time blocks.

A time block is where you set aside in your diary a block of time to work on a particular area of work. I use time blocks all of the time and it does enable me to get more done. One of the reasons it does this is because I get in the flow. If I have a time block for writing (which is currently Wednesday between 10.30 and 2.30) I am able to get in a writing flow. I eliminate distractions such as Twitter, LinkedIn, YouTube or email and have an outcome in mind for that specific time block. When I was writing this book I set aside a time block and had a target of producing 5000 words.

How could you implement time blocks? Just decide some result that you are looking for or a goal you would like to achieve and look ahead in your diary. Set a time block to work on that task and ring fence that time. You will be amazed at the difference this will make. If someone is asking for an appointment and you have a task already in your diary, more often than not you will be able to find an alternative time. The point is that you are proactively planning so that you can deliver a result rather than being reactive and fitting things in when you have 5 minutes. Your time blocks could just be 1 hour; if you work consistently on a single task for 59 minutes and stay on track you'll be surprised what is possible.

To summarize planning ensure you do these seven things:

1. Plan at least 1 week at a time.

2. Whenever possible plan your upcoming week at the end of your current week.

3. Focus on a certain Core Objective and then the goals to achieve that Core Objective.

4. Identify the tasks that are needed to complete a goal(s) and create three VITs for each day.

5. Develop a successful routine to start and end the day, then to start and end the week.

6. Introduce time blocks to work on tasks in a productive way and manage your distractions.

7. Remember that next week and next month are already there in your diary.

How do some people stay focused?

A key component of being personally organized is developing the ability to stay focused. The importance of focus and being consistent should never ever be underestimated. There was no way I could have finished my Triathlon or this book if I hadn't maintained my focus with my training. Wanting to complete the race in under 17 hours wasn't enough, I have to focus on doing the training consistently every single day.

In my business I have developed a simple habit that has enabled me to be focused. I have realized that many people in business have lots of things to do. In fact, it seems that being overwhelmed at least some of the time is a prerequisite of running a small business. The key is to focus on what matters. When you are in the day-to-day thrust of running a small business there will come times when there are things that need to be done. These are the critical things that will shape your future; often they are the key things that will ultimately deliver your Vision.

The key is to focus on what matters.

But here's the kicker: at the precise moment you know you should do this thing you can easily find something else to do that is more enjoyable, possibly easier and certainly more comfortable. Nearly always this other thing will make you feel better right now; it will give you almost immediate satisfaction. This is the CMD that Dr Tom Barratt talks about – your 'critical moment of decision'. What you do at this point is central to the life you're going to experience. If you do the easy thing that makes you feel good now, you're selling yourself short. If you do the important thing that will make you feel uncomfortable, you'll make progress but that's harder. The simple habit that I have developed is that I focus really hard on the outcome I'll get from doing the hard thing. I used to focus on the actual activity. When you focus on an activity such as going for that 6-mile run when it's cold and dark you don't want to do it. But when you focus on the outcome of what you'll feel like breaking 40 minutes at your next 10k or having the energy to play football with your kids in the park when you're 50, you'll take the right action.

In your business you are going to be faced with lots of tasks that are going to make you uncomfortable. Running your business is not going to be fun all of the time. But at that moment when you could do the easy thing or drift off and waste your time, if you can connect with the outcome of completing the stretch thing you'll find staying focused is much easier. This is why it's best to read your Vision every week; you'll keep it firmly in mind. That's why you are doing these stretch things because that's where you're heading.

Prioritize the major tasks so you make progress

The next thing that people do who are personally organized is work on what is important, not the stuff that is urgent.

Jim Rohn said: 'some people major on the minor things'.

One of the major reasons why people say to me 'I didn't have time to do that' or 'I don't have time to achieve that' is because they hop from task to task and allow themselves to be distracted and chase bright blue butterflies. Here's that revelation again: we obviously have enough time, which is why the day is 24 hours long. If we needed more time the day would be 30 hours long!

From now on, don't think you don't have the time, just think: you don't have the time to do all of the stuff you are doing that may not be enabling you to be your best. Stop some of the stuff that you are allowing to distract you from your plan.

The great thing for you is that now you have your **Stop some of the stuff** 1-3-5 Action Plan. This means that you have identified **that you are allowing** the important stuff that needs to be done for you to **to distract you from** reach your Vision. A simple rule that I apply to situa- **your plan.** tions where I feel I may go off track too much is to ask myself 'will doing this task take me closer to my Vision?' If it will, then it is important; if it won't, I may still do it at some point but not until the important stuff is done first.

I think the classic time matrix makes this point perfectly:

1 Urgent + Important	2 Important not urgent
3 Urgent + not important	4 Not urgent + not important

When I show them this time matrix most people agree that they should be working in quadrant 1, where they work on the things that are both urgent and important. But the best quadrant to be working in is quadrant 2 because you're working on the things that are important to you in reaching your Vision BEFORE they become urgent. When you are in quadrant 1 your back is up against the wall. You're under pressure and you will be working with a great deal of stress. Too much stress over a long period of time can be counterproductive. I understand that a little stress can make us step up a gear and perform better, but if it's all the time and we feel we're fire-fighting, jumping from urgent thing to urgent thing, then we're not being effective. A condition that many endurance athletes have to be aware of is overtraining. When you place the body under too much stress for too long you end up wiped out or injured. Both these will stop you training and cause you to lose condition. Remember that consistency is key, so manage your level of stress by planning your time better and getting yourself out of quadrant 1 and over to quadrant

2 where you can produce better results in a more relaxed environment where you take regular breaks.

If you work as part of a team you have to be careful about quadrant 3. This is where normally someone else makes something urgent, but to be honest it is not important to your reaching your Vision. Have your guard up and be prepared to say no; if someone else's bad planning drags you to quadrant 3 to help them out, it will mean you're not working on your important stuff.

Finally, we have quadrant 4. You probably could list some of the stuff you're currently doing and if you are not careful you could be spending lots of time on stuff that is neither urgent nor important. Beware of this quadrant and avoid operating in it. You're not going to be making progress here and there's no reason to be spending any time in here.

We've talked already about the importance of building successful habits. One of the ones you could work on is building the habit of being aware of which quadrant you're in and getting yourself into quadrant 2 more of the time. The first habit Stephen Covey shares in his book is Be Proactive. Being proactive is about acting before you're acted upon. Be clear about what is important to you and your business and do this stuff before it becomes urgent. A client of mine is building the habit of being early for everything; how simple is that?

When I first learned about the time matrix I spent a little time listing some of the tasks that belonged to each of the quadrants. I found that this helped me to identify them once the day and week started. This will work for you too.

People who get more done are consistent

Let's be honest for a moment. You know deep down that when you have let time slip through your hands and at the end of the day you've looked and said to yourself 'I could have done more' it was because you weren't consistent. You weren't sticking to what you should have been doing – you drifted off.

The great thing with consistency is that when you decide to be consistent you immediately see the results. It's like magic how your results immediately improve. When you're training for a big endurance event like a Triathlon, being consistent is key. It's not just important to do some big 3-, 4- and even 5-hour sessions. What is key is that you do your sessions consistently. Even if you started running and built up your time on your feet by 10% each week (a guide many people follow, me included), in no time at all you'd progress from a 30-minute slow jog to an hour of good running. This would only take you about 8 weeks of running. But what happens in the real world is people jog 30 minutes for a few weeks, don't make any progress, stop for a few weeks, waste time in front of the TV instead of being consistent and then decide they can't do the 10 k charity run. They then talk about themselves negatively using that evidence to confirm a poor picture of themselves, which confirms they can't run.

For you to be different, get clear about what you are going to do each day and reward yourself for your little breakthroughs. Keep a picture in your mind of what your outcome, your Vision, is going to be and commit to doing some of the things that just need to be done. If you were running don't go out and do an hour straight away, build up over time. The tortoise always wins the race because the tortoise sticks at it. To make the most of your time keep plugging away at your important stuff, keep yourself engaged with your future and just deliver. We've talked already about time blocks. Time blocks really do work. I've used them and I continue to use them. When you plan your week and your month and you identify some of the key tasks that are going to enable you to make progress, commit to doing it consistently. If a Friday afternoon at 4.30pm is time to reflect and plan the upcoming week, be consistent. If on a Monday morning you are going to read your 1-3-5 Action Plan, be consistent. If you are to make the absolute most of your potential and your 86,400 seconds every day, be consistent!

Are you being distracted?

Using your time effectively means managing your distractions.

We've talked above about being consistent. One of the easiest ways of not being consistent is to allow distractions. What distracts you? For me it was phone calls when I didn't want them, continually checking emails and having social media switched on all the time.

Write down three things that distracted you already this week:

1 _____

2 _____

3 _____

Look at these with a fresh pair of eyes. What could you do to manage these distractions so that you were able to remain consistent? For me I switched my phone to silent for large chunks of the day, maybe you could get your calls screened, run though a PA or call answering service. I only check my email four times a day and never ever before I have a plan of what I'm going to achieve that day. If you start your day with checking email I guarantee you'll build the habit of being reactive to urgent demands and find yourself in quadrant 2. Plan your day, be clear about what you want to have happen and then check your email. Finally, with social media I use Twitter, LinkedIn and Facebook at planned times. Have you noticed how easy it is to lose 40 minutes or more by checking your newsfeed and then on occasion watch that funny video? You know deep down there are more important things to do. Now I disconnect from social media and focus on being consistent. I then reward myself after producing some excellent work with a break.

What can you do to right now to address your three distractions? What new little process can you implement that manages your distractions? When I was writing this book, I left my office, went to a quiet place in the local university library and achieved far more. I have one client that rents a hot desk for the day when she wants to work on rather than in her business (working ON your business is where you work to improve and make it more effective, whereas working IN your business is where you work on the delivery of your product or service. To keep improving your business it is essential that you plan time and work ON your business). Again she makes massive progress that day. Another simply closes the door. If it's shut, her team knows that she is working on a task and does not want to be disturbed. For other clients they have allowed unrealistically high expectations to creep in from their customers. They are allowing themselves to be constantly distracted with phone calls about queries. We spent some time putting together some frequently asked questions and 'cheat sheets' for one of my clients. These pdfs were uploaded to their website and we then educated their customers to look there first for their query. We measured a large reduction in unnecessary calls and as a result my client was more consistent and made better use of their time.

I have found that by identifying the things that cause me to be distracted and addressing them is a very easy way to get more done. It has also meant that because I'm more effective with my time, I can have weekends off.

Key Development Point

Time-effective people have a clear picture.

You have already worked hard and clarified your Vision. Your Vision may be 3 years out or it may be 5 years out. Time-effective people have a clear picture of what they want to achieve in the shorter term too. This is similar to planning a long trip around the world; you'll have destinations en route that you want to visit. These mid-way points help to keep you on track. When you apply the same principle to your time in your business and life you'll find you are more effective. Part of my Monday success routine is to have a clear picture of what outcome I want for the week. I decide what success looks like on Friday night. I don't spend hours on this, I just clarify the progress that I would like to make and then on Friday I review my week and congratulate myself for the progress I have made.

I know for certain that because of this picture I can identify from my goals the tasks that need to be completed. I know for certain that because I can identify these tasks I focus on them and I'm consistent. I know for certain that because I'm consistent on these tasks I manage my distractions because I have an outcome in mind.

When I see people not using their time effectively I also see a person who isn't sure what they should be doing. Be clear what outcome you want for each day, be clear what outcome you want for each week and month. Once you have the outcome that is driven from your 1-3-5 Action Plan you will realize that you are on a mission. When you are on a mission you don't want to waste time. You have a purpose and your purpose is to achieve your Vision so that you can have the life and business that you want and you deserve.

Your progress so far

By this point you're getting more and more comfortable with your 1-3-5 Action Plan. You're a better leader and are focusing on what needs to be done and don't always give in to your emotions in the here and now. After this section, you'll understand how some people get more done than others. You are now armed with some excellent tools to make the most of your 86,400 seconds. You have built a clear picture, and you manage your distractions so that you can be consistent. You have also worked out what is important to you and you focus on those important things. You are starting to plan more effectively and you plan your day, week and month with those key things that are driven from your 1-3-5. You are developing that into a successful habit and you have made a decision to be personally organized and will give yourself the ideal environment to achieve your 1-3-5. Your confidence will be growing as you now have a plan to achieve your Vision, you have leadership skills to identify the right things to work on and now you are 25% more effective with your time because you have upgraded your skills.

!₀ Key Development Point

Set a short time block each week to review what you've done and plan what you are going to achieve the next week. Be disciplined with this.

9

Skill Three: Relationship Building

You've probably heard the saying 'Focus on the relationship and not the transaction'. It is always about the relationship.

For you to reach your Vision in your 1-3-5 Action Plan and make the most of yourself, you are going to have to focus on relationships with your clients and those around you. You are going to have to adopt the mindset of continuously looking for ways to enhance, strengthen and develop those relationships. The reason for this is clear. There will be others out there who also have a great product like yours. There will be others out there who will also deliver a great customer experience and there will be others out there whose product or service will also give great results. For you to stand out you'll have to do these three things and one more critical thing.

It's always about the relationship

Before we get to the critical thing, let's start with the basics. Too many business owners are making serious mistakes when it comes to managing the relationship with their clients. The key point to remember in this section is value. It's about value and value is in the eye of the beholder. We don't buy on price, we buy on value. If we bought on price we would all be driving the cheapest car we could find and wearing the cheapest clothes. But we don't, we drive a car that we feel represents good value to us. That could be £3000, £10,000 or even £50,000. We attach a feeling of value to the price, the product or service that means something real to us and our emotions.

Assuming the customer was right for you in first place, you probably have never lost a customer due to price. You probably just didn't do a good enough job of communicating the value of what you have to the needs and wants of your customer. Maybe you didn't ask good enough questions to ascertain their needs. Maybe you didn't explain every aspect of your product or service to your prospect and because of this they didn't understand the value to their lives and business that your product or service would bring. Here's the kicker: if you didn't do this and you assumed they would know all about your product or service, then you have let them down. Here's another kicker: because you didn't do this well enough you let them down, they weren't able to make an 'informed decision' and they went to someone else who couldn't and possibly won't take care of them as well as you would. So how are you feeling now?

Value is key and communicating that value is key

There are four different levels of value and I want to explain these to you so that you have a clear idea of the levels to take your clients through.

Level 1 value – Product

The first level of value you deliver is with your product. If you have a good product and it delivers what it is supposed to deliver, then you will be adding value to your clients/customers. I'm expecting that the reason why you are reading this book about becoming Unstoppable is that you have a great product or service that adds value. But, when was the last time you looked at your product or service through the eyes of one of your customers? When did you last spend 20 minutes critically assessing your product and finding some ways to enhance your product? This is something that has really worked for me more recently with my group coaching product. I looked at the product from the eyes of my clients and came up with three ways in which it could be enhanced. It was particularly good because these enhancements had little cost impact to me but a great deal of benefit to my clients.

Looking at one of your products, spend 20 minutes now and come up with three ways in which it could be enhanced:

1 _____

2 _____

3 _____

Now that you have got at least one way in which it can be enhanced, describe how this will benefit your customer:

_____

_____

_____

So, now that we have a way in which your product can be enhanced and a clear benefit identified that your customer will experience, how are you going to communicate this extra value?

All too often I come across people who have great products and services, spend time and effort enhancing them but THEN keep those enhancements a secret!

Level 2 value – Experience

The next area of value that we can work on is the customer experience. This is an area that some companies excel at. They make this a major point of differentiation. In this space are companies like Disney and John Lewis. They value the experience of their customers as key. They are always looking at ways to add value to the experience. They deliver exceptional customer service and the customer certainly feels important. How would you rate the customer experience you deliver? Have you asked some of your ideal clients how they rate the experience? Have you asked your ideal clients what changes they would like to see in the experience? When you request feedback on how you improve the service you deliver so that your clients have a better experience, you really are moving up the value tree. It makes your clients feel special and it communicates that you are taking your business seriously.

Do you benchmark either yourself or your company? What I love about benchmarking is that you can benchmark part of a company operating in a completely different sector to you. When it comes to the customer experience, what can you learn from companies that are in a different sector? What can you implement to enhance the experience of your customers? In order to deliver a consistent level of service and customer experience, could you benchmark McDonald's systems file? What can you learn about customer service from Amazon?

So, at this point we have looked at improving our product or service and then communicating how this improvement will benefit our target market. We have looked at the customer experience from the eyes of our customers and we have looked at benchmarking our experience to other companies that may not be in our sector.

Level 3 value – Results

The next level of value we need to be aware of and make sure we communicate is the results level. This works especially well in a business to business (B2B) environment but will also work in a business to consumer (B2C) environment. How clear are you about the results your product or service delivers? When you are talking with your prospects, do you regularly share the results of your product or service? Are the results you deliver communicated in your newsletter, your blog or your social media posts? Do you regularly request testimonials from satisfied customers that can be shared as social proof that when people deal with your business they get a certain result?

These are basic things but they are not that common. It's possible that you think it is not good to blow your own trumpet. Going back to the very beginning, the first thing we do when we are becoming Unstoppable is clarify our Vision. We do this because it's imperative that we get an understanding of what success means to us and have clarity about what we want our lives and business to look like. For us to reach this Vision, we are going to need some people. These people are our customers. You are only going to make sales and profit if you help enough people get what they want. What they want is value and results. By measuring and then sharing these results you are enabling people to make informed decisions.

When these people who are your ideal prospects understand this value and results, then they will engage your business. When they engage your business you will help them and they will help you. I find it best to keep it as simple as possible.

If you don't do this already, come up with an easy way of measuring the results people experience by using your product or service. It's important here to emphasize that the results they experience may not always be tangible. I recently did an exercise where I wanted to understand the emotional results people experience from my coaching and develop-ment. I asked for feedback from my clients. I have to be transparent here and say that I was very surprised by what I learned. My ideal clients told me that they felt a great deal more confident in running their busi-nesses, which in turn had the added benefit of their setting bigger and bigger goals. Because of developing an Unstoppable system they were achieving these goals. As a consequence of this information I was able to share this with ideal prospects and attract business owners that saw value in having more confidence and then setting and achieving bigger and bigger goals.

This exercise also has the benefit of solidifying the journey that my clients had taken, so it was definitely win–win.

Value level number 3 measures the results your customers experience and shares this information (where appropriate) to enhance the relation-ship and add value to that relationship.

Level 4 value – Senior team member

The fourth and critical level of value that will really mean that you will have long-lasting relationships with your customers and clients is where you are seen by your client as part of their team or life. This is the level where the strength of the relationship is in the fact that they see you as integral. In a B2C environment you may be able to identify certain products where the relationship you have is so solid because of how you have integrated that product within your life. An example that springs to mind for some of my friends is satellite or cable TV. I don't have either. I don't actually have a TV (and haven't had a TV at home for 8 years at the time of writing). But for some of my friends TV is all important. They will happily spend (they would probably say invest) a fairly big sum on TV every single month and not have a structured savings plan. In a B2B environment (more of my focus), the key here is to be seen by your clients as an integral part of their management team. Here, an example would be you sending reports or case studies to your clients that will enable them to build their knowledge or handle a difficult challenge without you expecting them to invest any more with you. I've shared this with one of my engineering clients. They mapped out one of their processes so that their customer understood what happens in their yard. They also invited their customer to their premises to explain the process. This enabled them to operate more effectively and plan better. Clearly, by doing this my client is adding massive value to the relationship and is now regarded as an integral part of their customer's business. It is also interesting to note that this is a great way to generate referrals because of the value demonstrated and delivered.

I've sent reports regarding running an effective professional practice to my accountant clients. I've sent fresh ideas of simple marketing plans to my chiropractic clients. I've sent performance management processes to one of my printer clients to enable them to manage their team better. All of these resources were from third parties. I didn't claim 'credit' for these, they were purely sent to demonstrate how I value my clients. Naturally, this had a beneficial impact on our relationship.

If you can add value to your clients and customers and be seen as an integral part of their business or life, then you are in a great position to enjoy lifelong beneficial relationships.

To summarize, the four levels of value that you need to move through are:

Entry level – Product/service features itself

Next level – The customer experience

High level – The results your product/service delivers

Top level – Being seen as an integral part of their business or life, you become central to them and offer fresh ideas to them on a consistent basis.

Top level is the level of value that will lead to lifelong win–win relationships.

 Key Question

What can you do today that takes you one step further to building top level value?

We have covered the four different levels of value so that you can move up and experience lifelong relationships. There are some important strategies that you can employ to ensure that you are developing client relationships.

Follow-up

The first strategy I want to share with you is follow-up. A mistake some people make is that they see 'follow-up' as something to do occasionally and not make part of their business mindset. The problem is that customers and clients can go elsewhere so easily either physically or online. If your customers or clients don't feel loved, then you'll lose them.

The Rockefeller Corporation shows that 68% of customers leave your business because they think you do not care about them anymore! Follow-up is a simple way to demonstrate that you do care for and value them.

A mistake some people make is that they see 'follow-up' as something to do occasionally and not make part of their business mindset.

I bet you can recall a time when you have called or made an enquiry to a company and left a message asking for someone to call you back. How did you feel when no one called, let down I expect? It still amazes me that some companies do not call people back who have taken the time to enquire.

How about when someone has dealt with you and they have bought your product or service? Do you have a structured follow-up process that automatically kicks in when someone has become a customer? How do you ensure that your customers remember you and what your business does? How do you add value after the transaction? These are simple things that can easily be fixed.

Let's look at follow-up in more detail. First, after someone has dealt with your business.

What precisely happens when someone has paid you money for your product or service? How do you ensure that they are happy and satisfied? How do you find out if they have feedback that could help you improve your product or service? How do you find out if you can be of further service to them, or other people they know for that matter?

You could implement a simple process of, say, a newsletter that adds value, does not sell 90% of the time and enhances their use or experience of your product or service.

You could implement a feedback form like the one I shared earlier on where you ask your customer to rate your service from 1–10.

You could write them a letter (yes, a physical letter not an email, you'll stand out) and ask if they would like to come to a refresher day or taster workshop, which is free if they bring a friend.

You could send them a value-added blog for areas of interest to them.

When you begin to think, you can probably come up with loads of others. The point is that you have a simple, documented follow-up system in place after someone has become a customer or client.

Some of the follow-up strategies that are currently working for me are:

1. After someone downloads my free action book there is a series of emails (eight) that add value and ensure that the person is reading and utilizing the action book.

2. I have a newsletter, http://petewilkinson.com/subscribe, so that people get some fresh ideas and a bit of motivation on a monthly basis.

3. I regularly offer clients free client appreciation events where I share some new learning so that they keep developing.

4. Conduct a 90-day catch-up call after clients have finished a programme to ensure that they are still using their 1-3-5 Action Plan and address any sticking points.

5. Produce a range of valuable free resources for my clients so that they can share them with their family and friends to help people take action.

6. Send key actions from live sessions so that client progress is made.

I think you get the picture that I ensure that I follow up after someone has been a client of mine or invested in a product. I have developed this habit so that it is something that I consistently do. I do it because I value the relationship with my clients.

An example that I feel shows simple follow-up after delivery is Jet2.com. My father lives in Spain and we sometime fly out to see him. One year we flew over as a surprise for his 70th birthday. We flew with Jet2.com. I was very impressed when, in late January the year after, I received an email from them saying 'around this time last year you flew to Spain, we wanted to let you know about some of our deals in case you fancy a break again'. I remember thinking how simple this would be to do but how potentially powerful it could be. It's worth noting that we also do on occasion fly with another short haul airline and don't receive follow-up emails like the ones from Jet2.com.

I'm also a customer of Amazon and they follow up very well. They often send me valuable emails (which I can switch off if I want to) about what other people are reading or if they have any offers. They also request feedback on a purchase.

What can you do to follow up? How can you stay front of mind with your customers? Some of my follow-up strategies were very easy to implement.

Do you always follow up?

There is another mistake that some business owners make and I know for certain that this mistake is costing them £1000s.

The mistake is that many business owners only follow up after the delivery of their product or service; they don't follow up BEFORE the delivery.

This is major. If you want to start the client relationship on a nice solid foundation, then demonstrate value up front even before your prospect becomes a client.

You can do this in many ways. A great case study that worked for me concerns John. John had a business in the tourism field and regularly received enquiries from outside the UK where he was based. A normal chain of events was:

1. Suspect enquires through website about a destination.

2. Suspect then requests a quote or proposal and becomes a prospect.

3. Prospect receives a quote and a call to make sure everything is OK.

4. The trail stops there unless the prospect gets back in touch.

I think to be fair this is a similar story in many businesses.

This was beginning to frustrate John and luckily for him he had developed his Unstoppable system. We sat down and wrote a series of value-added emails (10 in total) that were loaded onto an auto responder (an automatic way of sending emails) that were sent at prescribed intervals. We spent a lot of time getting the subject line right, which is absolutely key. It's worth pointing out here that it's ideal to test and measure different headings. Each email was built on the previous one and 'coached' the prospect to realize that if they were considering travelling to the UK that we should be the business that they selected. We covered topics such as fundraising ideas to contribute to the cost of the trip, what you should do when visiting the UK, things to pack in your case last minute, etc.

In no time at all an amazing thing happened. By email six there was a great increase in the number of prospects getting back in touch with our company. The result was that we experienced a 35% uplift in sales. Because of this, John bought a new car as a reward and moved to a more suitable and prestigious office.

What can you do to demonstrate your value up front before your prospects become clients? It is a great mindset to develop and will bring excellent dividends.

What can you do to demonstrate your value up front before your prospects become clients?

From my experience, follow-up is something that businesses do occasionally that they should do consistently. In order for you to do follow-up on a consistent basis I'd like to share a three-stage process I learned years ago while doing my MBA.

The three-stage process involves:

1. Unfreezing what you are doing now. If you have a habit of not following up and leaving your clients hanging in limbo, you have to unfreeze that practice.

2. You then put in place the change itself (every bad habit needs to be replaced with a good habit). It helps to start small and build once you have become consistent. With follow-up it could be simply putting an entry in your diary 30 days after your delivery date and making a short follow-up call to make sure your client is happy. If you deal with big numbers, automate this. We did this when I had my retail business. We religiously called every customer after delivery to make sure everything was OK; they certainly felt valued.

3. This is the essential bit. You have to refreeze the change process as the newly established process; you'll need total focus at this stage. What I mean by this is you have to own this change and ensure that it happens. This is where many companies fall down. They stop what they are doing, they put the change in place and then for a while stick to it. But after a short while they go back to their old ways.

Maybe you have done this before. You must absolutely commit to refreezing the new process of follow-up. Do regular checks to ensure it keeps happening. This is why it is worth starting small to begin with and then building from there.

Lifetime value

Another strategy that I want to share with you, which is a little simpler and easier to implement than follow-up but can also contribute to the customer relationship, is lifetime value. All too often companies only work on the value of their customers by their initial purchase. Let's say my wife gets her hair done every 6 weeks. She tells me it only costs £50, I expect it's a little more than that. But let suppose she's telling me the truth (I'm saying that because to be fair I may have misled her in the past about how much my carbon fibre race bike was). If Sharon spends £50 every 6 weeks she is going to spend about £430 a year. If she goes to the same hairdresser for about 5 years, then the lifetime value of Sharon to the hairdresser is over £2000. When you work out this lifetime value for your clients in your business you may be surprised by the figure. When you know that real figure you may be more inclined to add value to strengthen the relationship and fully appreciate the impact your customers are having on your business.

In short:

1. Work out the initial purchase value.

2. Work out how many times a year they purchase from you.

3. Work out on average how long clients stay with you.

This lifetime value figure is not only important when you consider developing client relationships, it's also very important when you consider your marketing budget for attracting your ideal client.

Satisfied and loyal customers are not the same

Realizing that satisfied and loyal customers were not the same was a revelation for me. If you are satisfied you may go back and deal with that business but you're not guaranteed to do so. If you are satisfied you certainly will not be an ambassador for the business.

In our small businesses it's very important for us to find ways of developing our satisfied customers into loyal customers and then into raving fans. If I take my wife for a meal and the meal comes on time, it is what we ordered and the food tastes nice, I would be satisfied. I expect that anyway, but that would not be enough for me to become loyal. For me to be loyal and then a raving fan, the restaurant has to do something extra.

An example I experienced recently was with iTunes. I was looking to buy an album and selected the one I wanted – it was £7.99. Just before I clicked to buy it iTunes popped up with a message saying that I already had three songs from this album and I could click another button that was to 'complete my album'. I did that and only had to pay £6.02. WOW! How good is that? Letting me have the album I want at a price I'm happy with will make me satisfied. But letting me know that I already have some of the songs and then saving me money and compiling the album for me is certainly moving me right up to loyal, and then on to raving fan!

Key Question

What can you do to develop your customers and clients into raving fans?

We've already looked at some follow-up strategies and you may come up with something there. Maybe it's about top level value so they see you as an integral part of the team. The key is to realize that satisfied customers are not enough; you need loyal customers and then raving fans.

How do you know when you have raving fans? Well, a raving fan is someone who actively wants to see your business improve. Remember when we talked about building a reputation? One of the key parts to building a reputation is to promote what others say about you. Well, when you have exceptional service and deliver top level value, then your loyal customers will go around and become ambassadors of your business, they'll promote your business for you. You'll know they are doing this by the referrals or enquiries you receive from interested people.

When you value your client relationships, then you'll follow up with these people properly and develop a relationship with them where you demonstrate value up front.

That's a great place to be; you'll receive leads and opportunities generated by your clients. How good is that going to be?

Key Development Point

It's not about the transaction, it's about the relationship, it's always about the relationship. Are your client relationships strong enough?

10

Skill Four: Key Strength Development

I'm sure you have many strengths. I'm sure there are loads of things that you do really well. Do you know what they are? Seriously, do you know what they are? Then there will be your weaknesses, the things you work hard on improving that you are really not very good at. You know what? That's OK, it really is. I've been fortunate enough to have worked with many leaders from many different businesses and the one thing I always notice is that none of them could do everything. In fact, the really good ones surrounded themselves with people that were better than they were and then led them and motivated them to produce a far better result than the leader could do by themselves.

A large part of being an effective business owner is to understand what you can do and what you can't do and focus on what you can do. I know this sounds simple and being successful usually is. We often miss the obvious stuff by looking really deep for a more complex answer.

We often miss the obvious stuff by looking really deep for a more complex answer.

I've been told in the past to work on my weaknesses. From my experience I've found that is the wrong thing to do. Sure, in your personal relationships you may want to develop your personal skills to be a better husband, wife, partner or parent. But it is different in business. In order to be successful and run a successful business you really need to focus on your strengths and find ways to manage or delegate your weaknesses.

In fact, in order to make this point let me give you an example. My background is retail, specifically electrical retail. I was good at it and ran my own business fairly successfully for 6 years. But being a successful retailer required many skills and, to be honest, some of those skills to be exceptional or world class I lacked. Because of this I realized that I was never going to reach the level of success I wanted in that particular business. When I launched my speaking and coaching business I realized at the outset (I thought long and hard about it and took some time out) that the skills I have are perfectly suited to speaking and coaching and that motivating, inspiring and enthusing people to work at a higher level is something I excel at. I could have stayed in my old business and continued to do fairly well, but I wouldn't have excelled. In that business I wasn't making the most of myself.

It's the same with my triathlon and cycling. I do better in the longer events, the events where my very high energy levels and ability to sustain a high endurance level for a long period of time are required. In shorter sprint events it's more about power for a shorter period. Riding flat out for 12 miles in a sprint triathlon is not my bag, but going for 50 or more miles over lots of hills is.

To jump slightly off page here, I think it's worth pointing out the similarities between Ultra Endurance and running a business. An Ultra Endurance Triathlon is a mammoth task; it could take you up to 17 hours to complete. Even working at a desk or in your business for 17 hours straight would be a challenge but try moving non-stop from 6am in the morning to 11pm at night and you get the picture of what an Ultra Endurance Triathlon is about. It is an endurance event where being focused and consistent is key. Isn't that like running your business? Isn't running a business and having an effective life about being focused on the right things, being consistent and putting in a big effort for a long period of time?

Launching a new business, a new product or even competing in a new market will require you to be focused and consistent. You won't be finished in a few months, you'll have to stay on track and stick with the plan to get the result you require.

Look at the business you are in now. Is it right for you? Does it fit you? You can still work really hard in your current business while you get yourself in a position to move into the right business if you need to.

Now, when I work in my current business I'm in a flow. I'm playing to my strengths and achieving results that reflect that. I'm not going to say that it's always easy, it's not. I've said before that some stuff just has to be done and by taking emotions out of it you can do that stuff. But to give yourself the best chance overall of being successful, make sure you're in the right business.

What are your strengths?

Have you ever worked out what your key strengths are? It's not something people often do; it can be quite difficult especially if you don't like to sing your own praises. I believe that it is very important to work out what your key strengths are and build your business around them.

There's nothing worse than running your business and having some underutilized strengths. You really do not want redundant skills to be floating around inside your business.

How do you find your strengths?

There are various structured ways to find your strengths and preferred way of working. Some of the ones that I've experienced are Belbin, Myers Briggs and Insights. These are great tools and can be investigated separately. For the purpose of this section, I suggest you start to make progress by answering some basic questions to get an understanding of what your strengths are.

When I began to work out my strengths I asked many people who I'd worked with in the past what they thought I was good at. You have to be careful here and be prepared to hear things that may surprise you.

The first step to take is to ask five people who you have either worked with closely in the past or who you work with now what they think your three key skills are. I feel that asking for feedback from those around us is very important and a great way to make consistent development. We need to be open to feedback.

Hopefully, after you've asked these people you have some overlap answers.

The next step is to ask yourself what it is you think your three key skills are. Clues to this answer are going to be:

- The things you do easily.

- The things you don't put off.

- The things you really enjoy.

- The things that make you feel good.

- The things that you would do even if you weren't getting paid.

Be aware that just because you are interested in something, it may not be wise to build a business around it. I love triathlon but I'm never going to be a professional. Your strengths are things that you have a natural ability in, that you have been trained in, have experience in and are potentially world class at.

Your strengths are things that you have a natural ability in.

It's important to manage and delegate your weaknesses. For me paperwork is something that I put off. I often find something else to do instead of doing paperwork; as a result I have someone else to do it. However, if someone wants to chat with me about how they may become more focused and successful, I jump at the chance and make time. If my business involved loads of paperwork (it doesn't) I wouldn't enjoy it too much. It does involve talking and listening to people, enthusing them to perform better and sharing strategies to make that happen. Looking at the points above I find talking with people easy (even to very large groups). I never put that off, I really enjoy it, plus it makes me feel good. Finally, I always go the extra mile as a matter of course and always do more than I am paid for!

Over to you. Are you good at paperwork and numbers; my accountant clients spend all day with numbers? Do you love speaking with people? Do you love teaching? Do you love solving problems? Are you creative? Can you manage many projects? Do you love finishing things off or do you like to start things and then hand them over? Are you a people person or do you prefer to work alone? Do you like kids or prefer to work with adults? Do you like to use your mind or your hands in your work? Are you an office worker or do you prefer to be outdoors?

Looking more critically, are you a good communicator or do people often say you don't listen? Are you good at influencing people and sorting out tensions? Can you remain focused on a single task or do you lose concentration? Do you have an eye for detail or are you always thinking big picture?

At this stage, write here what you feel are your three key strengths after the feedback from your colleagues and answering the questions above:

My three key strengths are:

1 _____

2 _____

3 _____

Now some important questions for you to answer:

In your current business are you allowing yourself to fully utilize your three key strengths?

_____

_____

_____

What have you done in the past 6 months to develop either all or one of your three key strengths?

_____

_____

_____

What could you do today to make more use of one of your key strengths?

_____

_____

_____

What effect on your business would you experience when you did what you identified in the above question?

_____

_____

_____

There will be some things that you do that are world class. Hopefully, by doing these exercises you will have identified what they are. It's fair to say that your ultimate success and fulfilment will be linked directly to how much time each week you spend with your key strengths.

Let me tell you about a client I had a short while ago who was an IT consultant. He was extremely good at explaining how IT worked. His clients kept telling him that he made it sound so simple. If you've ever spent any time talking with an IT consultant you'll know how nice it would be if one of their key strengths was making it sound so simple that you understood what was going on.

When we started working on his key strengths he shared the feedback from his clients, and we agreed that there was one real key strength for him. After more dialogue I learned that he also loved teaching and explaining things. He was a member of a motor club and was interested in how mechanical things worked in general. So, after a little time we knew that he was great at explaining how IT worked and keeping it simple, plus he loved teaching and talking to groups. Here's the message: up to this point he had never thought of teaching IT to groups of people in a group environment so that they understood how to utilize IT better in their businesses. He had these key strengths and had never married them together. Imagine what could happen if he was able to spend time doing more of what he loved while developing another stream of income? This could be a major game changer for him and lead to massive business growth.

Wouldn't it be a real shame if you are in a similar place and have strengths that you are not making full use of?

Keep working on your strengths to go from good to great. In my business I have other experts supporting me with branding, key messages, product development, marketing and speaking. I'm pretty good at these things (being a bit modest here) but I regularly get input from people who can challenge me to develop my strengths further.

What are your weaknesses?

When I'm working with clients they find it much easier to answer this question than answering the same question about their strengths.

How about you? Could you find it easier to identify your weaknesses than your strengths? I normally have to reach deep inside to learn people's strengths but they can list loads of things that are their weaknesses. Is this faulty thinking? If we are working hard in developing our businesses to build the life and future that we want and deserve but most of our thinking is around what we are weak at not what we are strong at, we are selling ourselves short.

This needs to change. We need to identify what we are weak at and instead of working on these weaknesses we have to find creative ways of delegating our weaknesses. We have to find someone else who loves to do what we find a real struggle. I understand that in a small business maintaining a competitive cost base is key. But if you are taking 2–3 hours to do something to a reasonable level that someone else could do in 40 minutes and to a higher standard, you need to find a way of engaging this person. Virtual assistants are especially valuable in relation to this. I pass lots on to my virtual assistant. I use the time that I save to work on my strengths. I see many business owners doing all of the tasks in their businesses themselves even if they are not good at it. Michael E. Gerber makes a great point in his excellent book *The E-Myth* about not staying at the technician level. Allowing your business to grow through to the maturity stage of development is very important and it is how all great companies continue to grow.

Identifying your weaknesses

We're not going to spend too much time on this here but it is important for you to get an angle on the three main weaknesses that you have. It's important because I expect if you're like most small business owners and professionals, you are working in areas that you are weak at every week. Once you have identified your weaknesses you can go about coming up with creative ways in which to delegate these to someone else.

For me, I discovered that certain tasks in my business were taking me a lot of time and that I could find other people to do them for me. The main ones that I'm currently weak at that I'm getting support from others on are:

- My wife doing my bookkeeping.

- My virtual assistant doing my direct mail, welcome pack management and other repetitive admin tasks.

- A social media expert developing my online strategy with Twitter and LinkedIn (I still do all posts).

- My web guy building my landing pages and main website changes.

These four main things were taking up far too much time because I couldn't/wouldn't do them effectively.

When you identify what your three weaknesses are and then find a creative way for others to support you with these, you'll be flying. You really will feel a weight is lifted and in no time at all your business results will show that you're working in the areas you should be working in and not on the things you shouldn't be doing.

Key strengths of an effective leader

There are four keys strengths that an effective leader should have. These are the strengths that will enable you to lead effectively within your business and make the very best of yourself and your team. These four key strengths are:

1. Executing

2. Influencing

3. Relationship building

4. Strategic thinking

How would you rate yourself in these four areas?

1. Executing

Getting things done and carrying through with a project or an initiative is important. People don't like working within businesses where there are 10 things on the go but nothing is finished. You may not be a good completer/finisher, that's OK. The important thing is that you are able to make sure things are complete. Who can you get support from to make sure things are complete? Execution is similar to when we talked about delivery earlier on in the leadership section. Too many people fall down with execution. I find that when I really connect with the outcome of a project or initiative and I clarify what I will see, hear and feel, I'm far more inclined to execute and get things done that are uncomfortable. To be effective in your role as a business owner or professional, what can you do to get better at executing?

Key Question

Is there something you haven't finished that between you and me you admit needs sorting?

What can you do that by the same date next month you have executed and got this boxed off? How will you feel when you finally box it off? Come on, you can make a difference and change!

2. Influencing

OK, so this sometimes has negative connotations, some people see this as a dark art. For me, being able to influence others as long as the outcome is an ethical one is essential. Being able to influence your team so that they perform at a desired level is key. Being able to influence your customers and clients to realize that if they have a problem you can support them is very important. If you don't do a good job of influencing them and they go and deal with another business, receive poor service and don't get the same results, then you have let them down! Understand that in order to influence people you have to be a good communicator. We covered the four pillars of NLP earlier on; it may be a good idea to review these with the outcome of influencing in mind.

Key Question

Who would you like to influence and why? What can you do over the next 7 days to influence this person to perform or support you in a certain way?

3. Relationship building

We have already talked about building client relationships in great detail. In this area we're talking about also building relationships with your team and your other stakeholders. What are your relationships like with your shareholders (supposing you have them) or your suppliers? What are your relationships like with your team? What do you do on a regular basis to boost the relationships with your team? It's important here to remember that no one became successful by themselves and that we all need other people in our businesses and our lives. Being strong at building relationships is a way to build that support team so you reach your goals.

Key Question

In order to develop this strength who can you identify that you would like to build a stronger relationship with?

What can you find out about this person so that you may share some common ground?

4. Strategic thinking

Are you a strategic thinker? You'll remember when we talked about leadership in simple terms; it's about Future, Engage and Deliver. Your thinking as the business owner needs to be in the future. Being strategic is about looking ahead and deciding on a course of action. Thinking strategically is about building the big picture and not allowing yourself to get bogged down with the detail too much. How often do you look at your business from the seat of a helicopter? When did you last critically look at the direction your business was moving in? Is that the correct action or do you need to change course? For me, being a strategic thinker is about deciding on what is going to happen in your business, not sitting back one day and saying to yourself 'what happened there?' The whole purpose of developing your own 1-3-5 Action Plan is to enable you to think strategically about your business and life and follow a simple strategy to get you from where you are to where you want to be in a most effective manner.

What are you going to do to develop your strategic thinking skill?

 Key Question

Are you going to totally commit to reviewing your 1-3-5 Action Plan weekly?

Are you going to think further ahead? The sign of a good driver is that they don't just drive to the end of their bonnet, they look ahead down the street. All too often people just drive and only look ahead a few feet in front of their car. But if you look further down the road you can anticipate what might happen and make more effective progress when driving. It is like this in your life. Get better at looking further ahead.

The main takeaway for this component of strength development is to emphasize that it will be how you use your strengths in your business that will determine your success. Developing your weaknesses is not an effective way to develop your potential. If you're weak at something, find a way of managing or delegating it. If you're strong at something, think how you are utilizing that strength and also how are you going to develop that strength. There's a really good reason why Mo Farrah, the British runner, breaks records and doesn't compete in the deadlift. Think about it! Identify your strengths and make absolutely sure you are using them fully in your business.

 Key Development Point

It's vital that you build your business around your strengths and find way to manage and delegate your weaknesses.

Where you will be by now

We've come a good way so far. I'm pleased you're still with me. Let's review. You've covered the background and got a good feel of how I came up with the Unstoppable system. You've spent some time and developed your own 1-3-5 Action Plan. You're going to read this at least once a week, ideally on a Monday morning, to frame your week. In your 1-3-5 you have created a crystal clear succinct four to five sentence Vision as your definition of success that is clear, positive and personal. You now know what you're going to give, who you are going to give it to, what value they will receive and what you will get in return. You have got a good picture of the way that will enable you to live.

You have chunked down your Vision into 3 Core Objectives. You realize that many people go off track and do not operate consistently in their business. This is not going to be you. You are going to use your 3 Core Objectives that are core, specific and written like you've achieved them to keep you focused on what is important. You realize that if you work on your Core Objectives on a consistent basis you will make progress.

From the creation of your 3 Core Objectives you set 5 Goals for each Core Objective. Your goals are stepping stones, action orientated and outcome focused. Your goals are what you are doing to ensure you take daily action. You are going to identify your three very important things (VITs) every day to keep you engaged and motivated. You now know for sure that you'll be ahead by Friday night every week. This helps you to feel fulfilled and happy in your business.

In order for you to make the very most of your 1-3-5 Action Plan you have started to work on your skills. The four main execution skills you have been working on are Leadership, Personal Organization, Relationships and Strength Development.

Putting all of this together, you're going to fully develop your Unstoppable system so that you will Be Focused, Be Consistent and Be Exceptional.

You're now feeling motivated and inspired to make it all happen and have a fantastic year. Now we move into the final part of this book where we look ahead and apply the development that has taken place. Part Four is about the next 12 months and what you can do to ensure you have a fantastic year.

Part Four

The Next 12 Months

Wouldn't you love a process to ensure that the next 12 months are fantastic? Well, that's what we're going to cover here. I'm going to share a seven-step process that I and many of my clients have used.

You've come a really long way, you now have a foundation plan in place and you've upgraded your skills.

It's critical that we now look at the next step. Your Vision is for the next 3–5 years and you'll be excited about what you are going to achieve. We need to build on that and be absolutely certain that we have motivation to take action and the persistence to keep going even though at times it's going to get tough.

Here are the seven key steps that will ensure the next 12 months are fantastic.

Step 1 What's worked and what hasn't?

The first thing I do when I plan a new year in business is to look back at what has been working for me and what has not. It may sound simple but you know what? Most people don't do it!

So let's start with what hasn't worked; I want to get this stuff out of the way first. Be honest, what have you done in the last year or in the last 6 months that didn't work? What have you spent time on that didn't produce the desired result? Have your social media efforts produced a result? Do your blogs receive good comments? Did your business structure work for you last year or did it mean you put too many hours in each week? It's a good idea to come up with the things that aren't currently working for you and make a decision. Can you change them or get some training that will make them work or should you stop doing them altogether and try something else?

There is an NLP operating belief that springs to mind here:

If what you are doing isn't working do something different.

In the past I've done things that didn't work. I'm being honest here; until I actually stopped and reviewed my year I kept doing them for far too long. I was expecting the result to change; it didn't.

What are the things you're still doing that you should stop and do something different?

Right, now to the good stuff.

What are the things that you are doing now that are working? Is networking working for you? Is your marketing working for you? Are your customer relations working for you? Is your referral strategy working for you? Is your pricing structure working for you? Is your follow-up strategy working for you?

You will be doing many things that are working well for you and it's important to identify what they are. It's possible that you've lost sight of some of the positive results you're getting from what you have done. Let's identify the things that are working for you and celebrate your success. From a leadership point of view this is about recognizing the good things you do so that you and the team keep doing them.

 Key Development Point

Work out what is not working for you and stop doing it. Work out what is working for you and do more of it.

Step 2 Success for the next 12 months

There are some key areas in your life that you need to work out what success looks like to you. The purpose of doing this is to decide in 12 months' time what would be a good result in these areas. It's vital here that you think strategically; don't jump around from idea to idea.

- Health: What does health look like to you? How about exercise? How many times could you exercise? What would you want your health to look like in 12 months' time? Would you like a certain body weight or composition? Would you like to complete a certain physical challenge? How about nutrition? What will your diet look like in 12 months' time? What foods and drinks will you start or stop eating and drinking? In 12 months' time will you only drink coffee three times a week? Will you have an excellent diet 80% of the week and reward yourself 20% of the time?

● Wealth: What developments to your wealth would you like to see in 12 months' time? Would you like to have reduced your debt by a certain figure? Would you like to have started a structured wealth creation plan? Would you like to be earning a certain income? Will you be saving a certain percentage of your income every month? If wealth is important to you will you have read three books on developing wealth?

● Family: How much time do you want to spend with your family? Do you want your family to grow in the next 12 months? Do you want to have special time with your spouse? Do you want to have a weekend away every 6 weeks? Do you want to support your kids to join a new club or team?

● Relationships: Which relationships do you want to develop in the next 12 months? Who do you want to attract into your support network in the next 12 months? Will you visit that old friend within the next 12 months? Who do you want to spend less time with in the next 12 months?

● Contribution: Where would you like to make a contribution in the next 12 months? How much money will you give to charity? Which voluntary organization will you give some time to? Will you look to identify a mentee to support and help?

It would be a great idea to come up with even one goal for each of the five areas above. The reason we're doing this is so that you achieve success in all areas of your life and become balanced rather than just becoming a motivated business professional only. Unless of course you want to, but from my experience being balanced and happy is the best place to be.

Now, we're going to look in more detail at your business success for the next 12 months. After all, that is the main purpose of this book, to enable you to build a foundation and have a system that supports you to be focused, to be consistent and to be exceptional!

What does business success look like to you?

I know it's a fairly big question but I find that having a 1-3-5 Action Plan is great and it's even better to clarify success for the next 12 months. Here, we're moving ahead 12 months and imagining you sitting down with your partner or friend and discussing how you've had a brilliant year in business. How do you know it was a brilliant year? It would be good to answer these questions and come up with a number or result for the ones that are either relevant or the ones that resonate with you and your business:

- What sales figure did you deliver?

- How many customers or clients did you support?

- How many boxes did you shift?

- How many professional connectors do you now have a relationship with?

- What margin level did you achieve?

- What profit level did you achieve?

When you have entered a number or result for the questions that are relevant above, the next step is to come up with a simple method of tracking that result. For example, if you entered £100,000 as a sales target for the next 12 months, how much would that be each month? How and where will you record that figure? Do you have a system in place to easily identify that figure?

If margin level is very important to you, do you or your accountant measure your current margin levels? What can you do to increase your margin? Could you increase the value of what you offer to improve the price and then by maintaining a competitive cost base, see the improvements you require?

For you to experience a better result that you experienced last year something needs to change. We need to find out what that is. By clarifying what business success looks like to you and then working back from there to identify actions is a simple way of doing it. I realize that there is a lot here but when you focus on your crystal clear Vision for the next 3–5 years you'll agree that it's totally worth it.

By the end of Step 2 you'll have a clear idea of what success looks like to you for the next 12 months.

Step 3 Product review

Here, I'm talking about the products and services that you deliver within your business. If you're a manufacturer, it's the widgets you make; if you're a business coach, it's the coaching products you offer; or if you're an accountant, it's the reports you produce.

Quick product overview

The first part of this is to carry out a quick (really quick) overview of your product portfolio. If we were sitting down together 121 I'd ask you:

- How happy are you with the range of products you have?

Look at your range of products; is there a logical progression from one product to the next? If you are a manufacturer, are your customers happy with the range you offer? If you are a coach, do you have any branded products? If you are an accountant, have you developed a value added management information product?

Being honest, how would you rate your range of products? Is the range good enough to achieve the result you want for the next 12 months?

- What are the gaps in your product portfolio?

When I asked myself this question I realized that I had a gap in the high end team coaching product. I developed a product for coaching professional senior management teams of between two and five people. I have more recently developed a workshop-based product complete with workbook that is to be delivered to larger teams of people. These two products have helped me deliver significant growth and help more people in a structured way. How about you? Could you ask your clients and customers what product they would like to buy from you? Could you look at other people and companies that occupy your space and identify anything they are offering that you are not?

● Which products need to be updated?

How fresh are your products? Look at what you deliver with a new set of eyes, or even ask a member of your support network (you have built one haven't you?) to have a look over your products. One of the great things car manufacturers do is carefully watch the sales curve on models. They always have the next product ready and plan the introduction to keep the sales rising. This is one reason why Nissan UK saw a sales increase of £1 billion in a year. Nissan are constantly refreshing and updating their product range.

I looked at my group coaching product a short while back and found a few ways to update it. I added more valuable content, I included a work file and action sheets and introduced an accountability call in between the face to face sessions to ensure that clients kept on track and made progress to ensure that clients kept on track. All of these updates resulted in better value for my clients.

I'm sure if you look at your products that you can find some way to improve them. The outcome we're looking for here is that your customers get extra value from the updates you've made, which enable you to have your best year.

I did this exercise with a client recently and we updated the product they delivered, which happened to be chiropractic. We streamlined the products that were available to mainly three. He came up with names for each of the three stages. He designed a map to demonstrate to his clients where they were on the map and which product would benefit them the most. There is a clear investment for each stage. His clients know where they are on their chiropractic journey and the investment required for each stage is really clear. He has experienced great benefit from doing this and his clients appreciate the simplicity; in his words 'it is a thing of beauty'.

- Which is your best performing product?

Of all the products you offer or the services you deliver, which is the best performing? Do you measure the performance of each product? It's important to understand which your hero product is.

When I had my retail business we had an electric fireplace that outsold all the others and that delivered an excellent margin figure. By measuring each product within the range, this included all departments such as laundry, refrigeration and television, we were able to ensure that the product was in stock and readily available for delivery. The whole department would suffer if that product couldn't be delivered. Looking ahead for the upcoming year, understanding your key product and driving it is essential.

- What makes this the best performing product?

Looking back at our fireplace, what made this a hero product was a combination of the style, the colour and the price. There was a formula that if we could replicate that to other products in the store they may experience the same level of success.

Now, I have a particular coaching product that is my best performing product. What makes this the best one is the combination of the results this product delivers along with the structure of the programme and the investment required by the target client base. This is the product that I need to spend time developing further and if time is limited this is the product that I need to promote.

The purpose of carrying out a quick product review is to understand that it is our products (I'm including your services here as well) that are going to deliver value to our clients. The results we deliver for our business will be directly impacted by the level of value we deliver to our clients. If we want to improve our results we need to improve our products.

Once you have carried out a quick product review you can move onto Step 4, which is people review.

Step 4 People review

I learned a long time ago that in order to become successful I couldn't do it by myself, I needed to have some other people in my team. In fact, I now believe that every business is a people business. Looking forward to achieving what is a massively successful year for you we have to review our team. Or, if you haven't got a team, build one!

I'm a micro-sized business professional; I don't have a traditional massive team of people that I employ. Even as a self-employed consultant or one-man band you will still benefit greatly from support from others. These other people could be trainers, coaches, mentors or members of your family. So, let's say you're looking for a certain result from your business this year, are there any knowledge gaps? Are there some skills that you simply don't have? If you are attempting to grow your business this year (hopefully you are) what support do you need and are the people you are currently working with the right people? It may be that the skills of your support team need upgrading.

You may be doing everything yourself in your business and I understand that it's important to maintain a competitive cost base. But if you could find someone to come on board in a creative way who could do a fabulous job for you, wouldn't that help?

As part of my people review for this year I recognized a gap in support from a mentor. At the start of the year I looked at the various parts of my business and in order to achieve major progress with Core Objective 3 I needed to raise my game. At the time I didn't have someone in my team that could push me in this way. I'm a member of the Entrepreneurs Forum and part of the benefit of being a member is the allocation of a mentor.

I met with the Forum and discussed my plans for this year. They allocated me a mentor who I contacted and shared my 1-3-5 Action Plan with. A long story cut short is that my mentor became part of my support team. He has supported me (and continues to do so, thanks Michael) with my Core Objective of developing my speaking business to a certain size. There is a great chapter in *Never Eat Alone* by Keith Ferrazzi titled 'Find mentors find mentees, repeat'. It is a great book anyway but I found that chapter very useful when I considered getting a mentor.

What can you do to ensure you have the right people in your team for this year? What action can you take to fill a skill gap or a development gap?

My speaking business wouldn't be where it is now unless I had carried out a people review and identified an area that needed developing.

A client of mine carried out a similar exercise but with a more permanent solution. We carried out a people review of his business and realized that he was doing certain tasks that, to be honest, he shouldn't have been doing. We looked at his workflow and the results that were being produced. Taking action he appointed a part-time assistant. WOW! The results were amazing. The amount of time this freed up was staggering. This individual, let's call her Julie, was a specialist in the area my client was weak. In her part-time role she revolutionized the back office and streamlined all the files and paperwork. She set up systems that meant loads of tasks didn't need to be manually repeated. Now my client, let's call him Peter, has a constant smile on his face as he's working on his key strength and what he was weak at has been delegated to Julie. As a result of this the business is growing. This all came from a people review.

You may be thinking that you are a small business owner and you don't have the resources to employ someone, even on a part-time basis. It may be that you don't want to employ someone. That's fine, you don't have to, but it's still worth carrying out a people review. You could find a creative way to skill swap. I know quite a few self-employed professionals who have done this. They've had support from other business professionals in a range of areas in return for their support. If you have a need for some people in your business to do a certain function or support you with a certain project, you can come up with some creative ways to get that support. After all, you have a crystal clear Vision of what you want your business and life to look like. Reconnect with your Vision, then find a way to get that support, the solution will be there.

Step 5 Time review

How well did you spend your time last year? Come on, rate your time usage effectiveness. I used to be about 5 out of 10. When I did my first year review and planned what I was going to do for the upcoming year I reviewed the things I spent the most time on. I realized that some activities had not produced a good enough result despite the time and effort I'd invested in them. I had spent too much time with prospects that were not ideal. Now I do a better job of assessing the 'fit' between us before we meet. I had allowed too many catch-up general chat meetings to take place where it was clear people only wanted to pick my brains for free and they were not going to change anything after our meeting. I now have a certain colour in my diary for general catch-up meetings and don't have more than two in a week. I had in the past been a little too opportunistic and spent too much time on projects that were not central to my strategy. Now I always practice outcome thinking and refer to my 1-3-5 Action Plan. If the activity will help me achieve one of my 3 Core Objectives I do it, if not I don't. I had also in the past spent too much time looking for things that I needed but were not at hand. Organizing my workspace has saved me a lot of time. I've been really honest there and given you some of the things that I came up with when I did my time review. Now it's your turn.

Key Development Point

Focus on the return you get from the energy you put in. Is it worth it?

If you go back to Chapter 10 you'll see that we discussed strength development in a bit of detail. The reason we did this is because you absolutely must make sure that your business is built around your strengths. That's the game you can win. Your strengths are probably very different to mine. When you look ahead at this year and assess how you use your time, the most important thing you can do is make sure you're spending most of your time working in the area of your strengths.

Make sure you're spending most of your time working in the area of your strengths.

Once you have built your business around your key strengths can you identify some of your weaknesses that you spend time on that are not serving you? Are there any activities that you regularly spend time on that are not giving you a good enough result? For this year to be the best year you've had, it's not going to be enough to have your 1-3-5 Action Plan. You have to assess your time usage so that you have the time to spend working on and with your 1-3-5.

Did you regularly use time blocks last year? How can you integrate them for this upcoming year?

Did you regularly plan more than a week in advance last year? How can you make better, more effective use of your diary this year?

Did you regularly use a master task list for the week driven from your goals last year? How can you work with a master weekly task list that is driven from the goals in your 1-3-5 Action Plan?

Who or what stole time from you last year? What are you going to do to limit your exposure to those people or situations this year?

What were the distractions that stole time from you last year? What are you going to do to manage those distractions this year?

All I want to do here is emphasize that before you embark on a new period of business or life development and planned growth, you should aim to stop and take stock of where you are and where you need to go. Improving the use of your time, working mainly on the things that are your strengths, is the most effective way to make progress.

The takeaway here is that the relationship you had with your time last year can change and you can easily become 25% more effective with your time. You'll have better results and be working fewer hours. That's the idea, isn't it?

Step 6 Message review

Here I want you to think about the messages that you communicate about yourself and your business. I believe we need to make a conscious decision about the messages we communicate.

How clear is the message you communicate right now? Could you tell me exactly what your message is?

Moving forward this year, what is going to be the key message you want to communicate? This message has to be clear and understood fully by your target audience, your client avatar. Your message should be written in your ideal client's language not yours. You've maybe heard the phrase 'message to market match'. This is what we are talking about here. For this year to be all that it is capable of, you need a message that is value driven so that your target audience hear it loud and clear.

Thinking about your target audience, how clear is your picture of who you are going to target this year? Do you know where they are geographically? Do you know what they are interested in? Do you know what sort of company or sector they are involved in? Are they in a certain age bracket? Is your target both men and women? Remember that if you are targeting everyone, then you are targeting no one.

What are some of the things that you want to communicate? For me, my message is about being focused and consistent and the transformation that will lead to better results. It's about how people can achieve more in a week than most do in a month by becoming Unstoppable. It's about supporting people to move from being 65% effective to more like 95%. It's about having more of those days when you're on top form and you produce results, and fewer of those busy days where you work hard but don't achieve anything. It's about having a senior team of directors or people working together to a central company-based 1-3-5 Action Plan rather than firing in different directions.

So, if that's the components of my message, I need to make sure that's what I am communicating. I understand that people are busy and have lots to do. Because of this I have limited time to share my message, which is why it needs to be clear.

What are some of the things you want to say this year with your business? Are you going to help people grow, develop and improve? Are you going to help them with their relationships, their life or their business? Are you going to make better widgets or service companies better? What do you want to be known for this year?

Make sure what you are doing day in, day out of every week this year is in line with your message. Often what we would like to communicate and what we actually communicate can be quite different. I'll give you an example. Recently, I was driving to Newcastle and when I leave home in Whitburn I have to drive through Cleadon. On one stretch of road the speed limit has been reduced to 20 mph. For the purposes of this example it's not important whether you think it should be 20 mph or not; stick with me.

Think about the message you want to communicate and the message you are actually communicating.

As I turned off the 30 mph road and onto the 20 mph road there was a car in front with a big sign in the back: 'careful, princess on board'. I reduced to 20 mph as the road passes a school, but the car in front accelerated to what looked like 35 mph judging by how fast it pulled away.

So, you have a driver with a 'watch out sticker' speeding past a school. Not exactly the message they were trying to communicate. I thought initially 'what's that about?' Then I began thinking about business and wondered how many businesses buy a sign, you could call it your marketing brand spend, and then do something totally different to what the sign says. They're missing out on lost profits and lots of business success and they aren't going to be building long-lasting strong relationships with their clients. Think about the message you want to communicate and the message you are actually communicating because without knowing it you could be doing 35 mph in a 20 mph zone!

Write the basis of your key message here for the upcoming year. Writing anything is better than leaving it blank; go on make a start.

_____

_____

_____

Once you have your clear message for this year and you strategically understand what it is you're going to communicate, we then need to look at how we're going to communicate it.

You could consider:

- Blogs

- E-books

- Reports

- Social media posts

- Webinars

- Website

- Letters

- Networking

- Workshops and seminars

- Testimonials

- Case studies

You can also look back at what has worked for you in the past and if can you do more of that. Networking has worked for me in the past, quite well actually. But when I got really clear about my message the results were far better. I also understood better which types of networking were more receptive to my message.

I've met some business owners that have many messages that are aimed at everyone. I know that if you have a clear message that is intended for a certain market, you will be more successful. This upcoming year get clear on your message and how you are going to communicate it.

Step 7 Actions

Thinking is good, talking is better, action is best! It all comes down to taking action.

So, in simple terms and with the outcome that you can make a difference straight away, here are seven actions for you to take:

1. What are three things that didn't work for you last year?

_____

_____

_____

2. What are three things that really worked for you last year?

_____

_____

_____

3. Have you got a clear picture of what business success looks like for the upcoming year?

_____

_____

_____

4. Have you carried out a product review and identified any improvements that need to be made?

_____

_____

_____

5. Do you have the right people in your team this year? Are there any gaps?

_____

_____

_____

6. Have you identified how to spend your time better and focus on your key strengths?

_____

_____

_____

7. Do you have a clear message for this upcoming year and know three ways in which you're going to share it?

_____

_____

_____

Completing these seven actions will be a major step forward in ensuring that this upcoming year is your best yet. The whole purpose of this last exercise is to get you to form the successful habit of reviewing your position every year. When you spend a little time looking at what worked well and what didn't and also assessing your products, your people, your time and your message, you'll be in an excellent position to maximize your strengths and multiply your results.

Remember, thinking is good, talking is better, action is best.

Conclusion

WOW! What a journey! I'm really over the moon that you have got to the end and gone through the whole Unstoppable system.

I realize that you may not have done all of the exercises but I urge you to do so. Whenever I carry out a follow-up review with my clients I notice a massive difference between two groups. The first group has had reasonable success and learned some cool new stuff. They've had a shot of motivation and they feel fairly good. Their results are quite good. Then there is the second group. This group threw themselves into the system. They did all of the tasks and took all of the actions. They have a crystal clear Vision of what they want to achieve. They have broken down their Vision into 3 Core Objectives so that they stay on track on a monthly basis and don't chase bright blue butterflies. They set their 5 stepping stone Goals that are dynamic and are replaced when they are achieved. They develop their leadership skills and review their habits, always developing a new habit every quarter. They make better use of their 86,400 seconds and plan at least a week in advance. They have strong relationships with their internal and external clients and continually look for ways to strengthen those relationships further by always adding more value. Finally, they build their business around their strengths. They realize that if they are to achieve their Vision of success they need to spend more time developing their strengths than working on their weaknesses to become average. They think strategically and above all use their 1-3-5 Action Plan to frame what they should be doing and review it every Monday.

My purpose is to help you to make the very most of yourself. I hope you've had a sense of that throughout my book. I'm above all massively passionate about you developing your Unstoppable system so that you can clarify and then reach your Vision. This system really works and will deliver fantastic results for you, but it is critical that you belong to the second group of people and do the work.

Running and working effectively in a business can be hugely rewarding and give you total freedom to live the way you want to live. Some things you do in your business will be fun; some things are hard work. Some things just have to be done. If you commit to developing your Unstoppable system I can guarantee that you will make more progress in a week than most people will do in a month.

I'd love to hear about the progress you have made. Let me know by emailing me at pete@petewilkinson.com.

I hope reading *Unstoppable* will be the start of your journey towards achieving exceptional results in life and business. To help you build on what you have learnt from this book, I hope you will access the free resources available from my website: www.petewilkinson.com.

They are designed to give you consistent, on-going support and advice, and to challenge you to achieve the highest level of success.

The fortnightly video blog will help you stay focused on your journey with tips, challenges and encouragement to keep you on track and the monthly 'Action Elite' newsletter will provide concise advice and information to help you review and consolidate your progress.

I really want you to succeed, so do the work and complete the actions. When you do you will be focused, you will be consistent and you will be exceptional. You see, that's what being unstoppable is all about.

Be *Unstoppable*,
Pete

About the Author

Author photo by Bec Hughes, House of Hues, www.thehouseofhues.com

Pete's professional career started 18 years ago with senior management roles in retail. Pete has managed a large team of 300 people along with having P&L responsibility for a £30m business. Pete has also run his own retail business with a much smaller team. He has an MBA from Newcastle Business School and is also an Ultra Endurance Triathlete.

Pete is massively passionate about ambitious, professional people achieving their potential and spends his time in his business delivering keynote presentations, leading workshops and partnering with chief executives and managing directors in a range of businesses from small micro-businesses up to multi-million pound larger organizations.

He is experiencing brilliant business success by using the strategies he presents on himself. He manages his time between his family and his business, and still competes in Ultra Endurance and long-distance cycle events.

Acknowledgements

This whole book has really tested me and my own system it teaches. I would not have been able to complete it without the help of my support team.

I'd like to thank the members of my Mastermind Team for their guidance, motivation and occasional bum kicking: Nicola Cook, Kennedy and Gary Candlish. I'm grateful for your support, guys.

I'd also like to thank the guys I train with who have kept things in perspective when we have been climbing steep hills or competing in events: Brian Anderson and Maurice Woodward. You two are the ones that keep me stretching physically and keep me grounded!

I want to thank the team at Capstone for their total support in helping me complete my first book.

Dan Bond also needs a mention as he has been with me from the start and pushed me to write a book in the first place.

Thanks again to Sharon, my gorgeous wife, who has managed everything else while allowing me to get tucked into my business and deliver key projects.